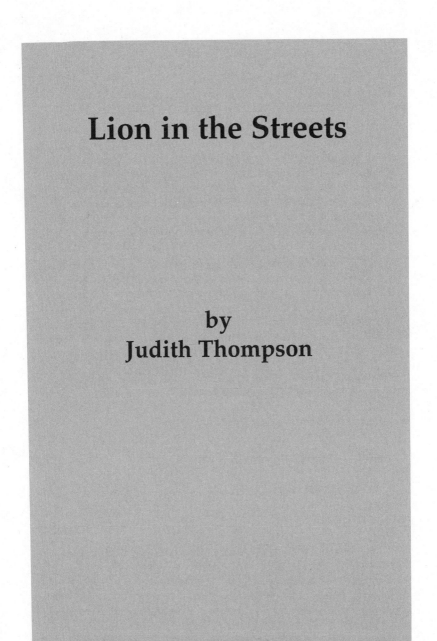

Lion in the Streets

by
Judith Thompson

Playwrights Canada Press
Toronto•Canada

Playwrights Canada Press operates with the generous assistance of The Canada Council, and the Ontario Arts Council.

Cover painting courtesy of Urjo Kareda.

Canadian Cataloguing in Publication Data
Thompson, Judith, 1954 —
        Lion in the streets
A play.
ISBN 0-88754-515-7
I. Title.
PS8589. H527L56 1996   C812'.54   C95-931989-4
PR9199.3.T56L56 1996

First edition: 1992 (Coach House Pres)
1st printing: October, 1996 (Playwrights Canada Press) ; 2nd printing: May 1997. Third printing, September 1998; Fourth printing, April 2000; Fifth Printing July 2001.
Printed and bound in Winnipeg, Manitoba, Canada - Hignell Printing Ltd..

This play is dedicated to the children in Seaton Village,
my neighbourhood in Toronto.

I would like to thank Gregor, Michael Ondaatje, Urjo Kareda,
Bob Wallace, all the actors in the cast lists, both Sarahs, and
Francesca, who held and rocked three-week-old Grace while
I transformed the hour-long radio play called "A Big White
Light" into *Lion in the Streets*. And, of course, Isobel.

The punctuation of this play carefully adheres to
the author's instruction.

During the extended six-week workshop in the Spring of 1990 that transformed Judith Thompson's radio play "A Big White Light" into the first stage version of *Lion in the Streets* at the duMaurier World Stage Theatre Festival in June 1990, Judith Thompson the director would occasionally ask the stage manager, Nancy Dryden, to break the company and dim the light in the small back space at Toronto's Tarragon Theatre where the workshop was being held. While actors and others drank coffee and ran lines in the lobby, Judith Thompson the writer walked about alone in the darkened room, getting into the blood, as she says, of her characters. By the time the break was over she would present, with astonishing rapidity, new, remarkable, and quite unexpected passages of text, often replacing brilliant lines or even whole scenes that, however effective in themselves, were deemed to be expendable. Great lines, she says, are a dime a dozen.

Quite apart from her alacrity in cutting, Judith Thompson's process as a writer is consistent with her background as a graduate in English from Queen's University and from the acting program of the National Theatre School, and congruent with Tarragon Theatre's reputation as the home of poetic naturalism. Her own training as an actor no doubt reinforced Thompson's well-developed sense of characterization and her acute ear for dialogue; and Tarragon Theatre has proven for almost a decade a congenial host for Thompson's writer-in-residency and a valued first producer for all but her first play.

But if poetic naturalism, however evocative, were all she wrote, Judith Thompson would not have the reputation she does as the creator of disturbing and dislocating theatrical experiences. *Lion in the Streets*, like all her plays, betrays an abiding interest in psychological motivation, and evokes immediate empathy for characters who are conceived in depth. Unlike those in more conventionally naturalistic plays, however, the characters in *Lion in the Streets* tend to be fragmented and discontinuous, and they are rarely contained within a single, unified action or linear plot. They tend, too, to be represented self-consciously as constructs undergoing crises of subjectivity, struggling to bridge a persistent gulf between the self that speaks and the self represented in that discourse as the subject, the "I." As the characters struggle to construct a *unified* self through a narrative that will allow them to understand—or "comprehend"—their lives, the play's plot becomes the site of duelling, contradictory, and even mutually exclusive narratives – multiple actions that are disturbingly open and exploratory rather than comfortably closed. This seems to be the case on the level of character and individual scene, in which the often violent or disjunctive actions are matched by a radical uncertainty about what is "really happening," about whose point of view is "true," and under what circumstances. But it is also the case that the overall "relay" structure of the play resists closure, containment, and easy comprehension, as a character from each scene is carried forward to the next, catalyst to a new action. As Thompson said, during a panel discussion at the duMaurier World Stage, "I just couldn't cope with the idea of a huge body of narrative... I started to find that kind of narrative tedious, because your expectations are usually fulfilled." Replacing the unity of traditional linear narrative are the overarching but problematic presence of Isobel, the play's collage-like composite portrait of an urban neighbourhood in crisis and, in production, a multiplicity of associative visual and musical linking devices such as the act-ending dances and the evocative disk that featured above centre-stage in the original duMaurier World Stage and Tarragon productions.

Naturalistic drama traditionally relies on the creation of fully empathetic characters whose psychological crises—constructed by the plays as personal neuroses—precipitate conflicts in the action. These conflicts are resolved through a "reversal" in the play's central and linear plot, producing in the central character(s) a "recognition" of an already existing, "well-adjusted," and unified "self" whose problems have been explained as deviations from a hegemonic social "norm." The empathy created between character and audience in such plays in turn produces a cathartic release of potentially disruptive emotions in an audience that leaves the theatre satisfied – calm of mind, all passion spent. Such plays, then, serve to contain potential social and psychological unrest, to explain disturbances and dissatisfactions in terms of individual psychology, and by purging discontent to affirm the social and political status quo.

In the plays of Judith Thompson, and most clearly in *Lion in the Streets*, intense empathy with naturalistically conceived character functions quite differently: in spite of a presentation of character that is psychologically acute, nothing is explained away. As she remarked at the duMaurier World Stage panel session, "I don't want to write industrial plays that play to psychology classes."

Thompson's characters experience a conflict between a self that is submissive to the inherited and hegemonic discursive practices of society and a self that is not synonymous with the subject of that discourse. The conflicts in *Lion in the Streets*, far from moving towards resolutions that leave characters and audiences satisfied that things must be as they are, present occasions for potential— and potentially redemptive—transformation. The audience is not allowed to settle comfortably into a single, consistent, or unified way of viewing or empathizing with the characters, to identify actor with character, to feel superior awareness to the characters, or to construct any but provisional narratives with which to contain and comprehend the action. And to the extent that the play invokes closure, it does so without authority; that is, it invites the audience to make sense, to take responsibility for the meanings and for the world that its members individually construct from their own distinct subject positions. At the conclusion of *Lion in the Streets*, the apotheosis of Isobel is nevertheless redemptive, not as a logical, natural, or inevitable outcome of the play's actions, but as an active exercise of will—or even faith—on the part of an audience that is urged to "take your life. I want you all to have your life."

Lion in the Streets is a profoundly disruptive, socially subversive, and deeply religious play. It revisions traditionally phallo- and logo-centric structures and languages, perverts the linearity of Aristotelian reversal and recognition, and replaces these with more radically contingent and consciously constructed shaping devices. And as in much feminist drama (as pointed out by Helene Keyssar in her book *Feminist Theatre*), the inevitability of reversal becomes in this play the possibility of transformation; recognition (of an already existing, unified subject) becomes the conscious selection of a subject position that is useful and meaningful in a particular context, and that allows audience members similar selection; and the experience of catharsis becomes the more unsettling but less enervating experience of fragmentation. Using the tools and intensity of psychological realism, *Lion in the Streets* dramatizes crises of subjectivity, and because its characters are characterized as constructs and presented as subjects in continuous process of construction, those crises are presented as providing for the possibility of change.

In spite of its realistic scenes of harrowing brutality and of ruthless emotional and intellectual honesty, the fracturing of subjectivity and revisioning of dramatic structure in *Lion in the Streets* are consistently used to insinuate the possibility of choosing and achieving "grace." And while the playwright sees "truth" as a passive state of tension, something that "happens to you through not doing anything," she posits "grace" in her unorthodox theology as the product of active human will, including the wills of audiences: "Truth," she says in an interview with Judith Rudakoff in *Fair Play*, "is simply what is... Grace is something you achieve. Through work. And Grace is something you have to work and work at. It happens through penitence, through sight. Through seeing who you are and changing things."

—Ric Knowles, March 1992

Ric Knowles is the author of *The Theatre of Form and the Production of Meaning: Contemporary Canadian Dramaturgies*. His introduction draws on material first published in *BRICK* 41 (Summer 1991).

Lion in the Streets was first produced as the inaugural Public Workshop Project at Tarragon Theatre in Toronto in May 1990, with the following cast:

ISOBEL	Tracy Wright
NELLIE, LAURA, ELAINE, CHRISTINE, SHERRY	Jane Spidell
RACHEL, LILY, RHONDA, ELLEN, SCARLETT	Ann Holloway
SCALATO, TIMMY, GEORGE, DAVID, RODNEY, BEN	Stephen Ouimette
MARTIN, ISOBEL'S FATHER, RON, FATHER HAYES, MICHAEL	Andrew Gillies
SUE, JILL, JOANNE, BECCA, JOAN	Maggie Huculak

Stage Manager	Nancy Dryden
Workshop Assistants	Urjo Kareda, Ric Knowles, Andy McKim
Set and Costume Design	Sue LePage
Music	Bill Thompson

Lion in the Streets received its world premiere at the duMaurier Theatre Centre as part of the duMaurier World Stage Theatre Festival in Toronto in June 1990, with the same cast.

Director	Judith Thompson
Set and Costume Design	Sue LePage
Sound Effects	Evan Turner
Lighting Design	Steven Hawkins
Stage Manager	Nancy Dryden
Production Assistants	Urjo Kareda, Ric Knowles, Andy McKim
Production Manager	Martin Zwicker
Set Construction	George Vasiliou
Wardrobe	Cheryl Mills
Properties	Mary Spyrakis
Apprentice A.S.M.	Henry Bertrand

Lion in the Streets subsequently was remounted with a revised text by Tarragon Theatre in Toronto, in November 1990, with the following cast:

ISOBEL	Tracy Wright
NELLIE, LAURA, CHRISTINE, SHERRY	Jane Spidell
RACHEL, LILY, RHONDA, ELLEN, SCARLETT	Ann Holloway
MARTIN, ISOBEL'S FATHER, GEORGE, MARIA, DAVID, MAN, RODNEY, BEN	Robert Persichini
SCALATO, TIMMY, BILL, RON, FATHER HAYES, MICHAEL, EDWARD	Julian Richings
SUE, JILL, JOANNE	Clare Coulter

Director	Judith Thompson
Set and Costume Design	Sue LePage
Lighting Design	Steven Hawkins
Composer and Performer	Bill Thompson
Sound Design	Evan Turner
Stage Manager	Nancy Dryden
Apprentice A.S.M. & Dance Captain	Nancy Katsof
Electrician	Patrick Hales
Sound Operator	John Alderman
Set Construction	George Vasiliou & Will Sutton
Scenic Painting	Gabriele Schnutgen & David Rayfield
Properties	Kate Hemblen
Wardrobe	Cheryl Mills & Sue Ward
Assistant Lighting Design	Paul Mathiesen
Waltz Coach	Viv Moore

This published text includes sections rewritten since the Tarragon premiere.

ACT I

The ghost of ISOBEL, a deranged and very ragged looking nine-year-old Portuguese girl, runs around and around in a large circle, to music, terrified of a remembered pursuer, in fact, the man who killed her in this playground seventeen years before the action of the play. There are autumn leaves all over the playground, and the kids who approach her all have large handfuls of leaves, which they throw at her. At this point ISOBEL does not know she is a ghost, but she knows that something is terribly wrong. She is terrified.

ISOBEL   Doan be scare. Doan be scare. (*turns to audience*) Doan be scare of this pickshur! This pickshur is niiiice, nice! I looove this pickshur, this pickshur is mine! (*gesturing behind her*) Is my house, is my street, is my park, is my people! You know me, you know me very hard! I live next house to you, with my brother and sisters, Maria, Luig, Carla and Romeo we play, we play with your girl, your boy, you know me, you know me very hard. But... when did tha be? Tha not be now! Tha not be today! I think tha be very long years ago I think I be old. I think I be very old. Is my house but is not my house is my street but is not my street my people is gone I am lost. I am lost. I AM LOOOOOOOOOOST!!

Four children—two girls and two boys—laugh and approach ISOBEL.

NELLIE   Take a bird why doncha?

RACHEL   Go back with the nutties to the nuttyhouse!

SCALATO   She looks like a crazy dog!

MARTIN   (*barks*) Hey!

All bark.

ISOBEL   Peoples! Peoples, little boy little girl peoples! Hey!

> *ISOBEL walks towards them.*

MARTIN   What's she doin?

NELLIE   She's coming over here!

RACHEL   She's gonna get us!

ISOBEL   You, girl, you help to me. I am lost you see! You help!

NELLIE   She smells.

RACHEL   You should dial 911 so the police could help you.

SCALATO   Where do you live?

MARTIN   With all the other pork and cheese west of Christie Street?

RACHEL   Martin that's not nice.

ISOBEL   (*overlapping*) Portuguese, Portuguese, yes... I catch a bus! Is there a bus, bus maybe? To take me to my home? You know a bus?

SCALATO   No buses here.

ISOBEL   Yah, bus right here, bus right here, number ten, eleven, I take with my mother to cleaning job, where this bus?

SCALATO   I said there's no buses here you ugly little SNOT.

ISOBEL   (*points*) You! YOU bad boy you bad boy say Isobel, BAD.

SCALATO   Why don't you get your ugly little face outa here, snot?

MARTIN   Snotface!

ISOBEL   Shut up boy, shut up, I kill you I kill you boy.

SCALATO   Hey she s gonna kill me!

RACHEL   She's a witch.

> *ISOBEL tosses rocks at them.*

MARTIN   She's throwin rocks! Hey she's throwin rocks!

NELLIE   STOP IT.

RACHEL   Stop throwin rocks or we'll tell the police!

ISOBEL   You BAD boy you BAD I will kill you!

SCALATO   (*jumping off and attacking her*) You just try it you goddamned faggot!! Faggot! Faggot!! (*hitting her*)

ISOBEL   (*growling like a dog*) G-r-r-r-r-r. G-r-r-r-r-r.

> *They circle one another.*

MARTIN   What's she doing?

NELLIE   I don't like her.

> *ISOBEL and SCALATO scrap and the others join in. SUE, a thirty-eight-year-old woman in a grey sweatsuit, walking home from a meeting, spies the fight and rushes up.*

SUE   Hey! Hey hey hey stop that right now! (*she pries them apart*) HEY! Listen! What is going on??

ISOBEL   I KILL YOU BOY!

SCALATO   She started it!

MARTIN   She was throwing rocks at us!

ROSE   She's crazy.

> *ISOBEL leaps towards SCALATO. SUE catches her, she falls to the ground.*

SUE   Little girl? Little girl!

ISOBEL   (*overlapping*) I kill that stupid boy.

SCALATO   She started it, lady.

MARTIN   I'm getting out of here.

SCALATO   Me too.

NELLIE & ROSE   Wait for me!!

SCALATO   You chicken, Martin! You suck!

ISOBEL   I kill that stupid boy! (*beat*) I no like those boys.

SUE   I'm sorry if they hurt you.

ISOBEL   They no want play with me. Why they no want play with me? Why all the kids no want play with Isobel? Ha?

SUE   Ohhh... sometimes kids are just... mean, that way, Isobel, when I was little kids were mean like that to me once.

ISOBEL   Kids? Mean no play to you?

SUE   That's right. We had just moved to a new town, Cornwall actually, near Montreal? Well my sisters and I went for a walk around the neighbourhood and these big boys on bikes started firing arrows at us.

ISOBEL   Boys on bikes?

SUE   That's right, just like those nasty boys!

ISOBEL   Nasty boys, to you, too! Mean to you!!

SUE	That's right. And those arrows, they hurt! They really hurt!! And I was the oldest so I told my sisters, "Just cry, just start to cry and then maybe they'll feel sorry for us," so we all started to cry.
ISOBEL	Cry.
SUE	But you know what? It didn't work! They kept shooting those arrows anyways. They were just mean.
ISOBEL	Mean boys shoot arrows. Haaah!
SUE	AND suddenly, a bigger boy, about sixteen, came along and made them stop, and you know, he was like an angel, to us, an angel who came down from the sky on his big blue bicycle I've never forgotten that.
ISOBEL	Never forgetting.
SUE	Nope. I guess I'm your helper today.
ISOBEL	Helper.
ISOBEL'S FATHER	(*on porch*) Hey! Is-o-bel.
SUE	Isobel is that your father?
ISOBEL	Father. My father. *Eu pensava que té tinha perdedo!*
ISOBEL'S FATHER	(*ordering ISOBEL to go around to the back door*) *Vai pela porta das traseiras.*
SUE	Hello.

ISOBEL'S FATHER grunts.

My name is Sue Winters and I don't know if you're aware of it, but some of the boys in the neighbourhood have been well I'd say doing some not very nice teasing of your daughter. I just... thought... you might...

ISOBEL'S FATHER goes in, slamming the door.

Poor man probably works all day in construction and then all night as a janitor in some Bay Street office building. What a life. (*she exits*)

ISOBEL My father? My father is not there. My father is dead. Yes, was killed by a subway many many years; it it breathed very hard push push over my father; push over to God. Hi my father.

Music. Lights come up just a bit. SUE is in her son TIMMY'S room, in the dark. TIMMY is in bed. ISOBEL watches.

SUE And so the giant starfish saved the drowning boy.

TIMMY What was the starfish's name?

SUE The starfish's name? Uh... Joey. It was Joey.

TIMMY Mummy? Why isn't magic true? I want magic to be true.

SUE Well. It is true, in a way, it...

TIMMY Not it's not. It's not true. And ya know what else?

SUE What, darling?

TIMMY I think tonight's the night.

SUE That what, Tim?

TIMMY That we're all gonna die. Tonight's the night we're gonna die.

Music. A dinner party, around a table. ISOBEL is there, invisible. The conversation is simultaneous.

LAURA   There was nothing to do! Nothing to bloody do but sing in the church choir!! And go to baked-bean suppers!! The snow at one point was actually up to the second-floor window.

BILL   No, she had the gall to ask my male students to, "Please leave the room," for her senior seminar. She did "not wish to be dominated by men." Where did that leave me, I asked her?

LILY   No, no no, you have to pat the dough, pat it for ohh a good five minutes then put it in the microwave for one, then take it out, then pat it again.

GEORGE   St. Paul said, "We are as vapour," what is it? Like "vapour vanisheth" or – something. "We are no more." So I got up this notion of Martians—being these—wisps of vapour... no, you see your problem is you want the aliens to be like you, you are anthropomorphizing, you...

LAURA   That's so boring. That's so knee-jerk boring.

BILL   And she launched into the most savage tirade–

> *SUE rushes in, dressed in her sweatsuit and sneakers. Everyone turns and freezes, except BILL, who continues to talk until SUE's third "Bill".*

SUE   Bill... Bill... Bill!! We have to talk!

BILL   Sue! Hi! Who's with the boys?

SUE   Mum came over, Bill I need to talk, NOW.

LAURA   Would you like a drink, Sue? We have...

GEORGE   Yeah, come in and sit down...

SUE   No, no thank you, I just... want to talk to my husband.

ISOBEL   My helper, Suuuuusan!

BILL	Oh – okay, Sue, I'll just finish this conversation. Anyway–
SUE	He thinks he's going to die.
BILL	Who?
SUE	Timmy! Your son! He–
BILL	What, did he say that tonight? Oh, that's just kids, he's–
SUE	BILL, come home, your son is very depressed his father is never there, why are you never never...
BILL	Sue PLEASE, we'll talk about it later, okay? So as I was saying, Laura...
SUE	Come with me.
BILL	I'll come in a while. I'll just finish this conversation, and then I'll come, okay?
SUE	YOU COME WITH ME NOW!
BILL	Sue.
SUE	Bill, I need you, please, why won't you come?
BILL	Why won't I come? Why won't I come? Because... (*he walks over to the others*) I'm... not... I am not coming home tonight.
SUE	Bill! Stop it, this is private–
BILL	It is not private, Sue, nothing we do is private for Christ's sake, you tell your friends everything, they all—know everything—about us, don't they? How many times we had sex in the last month.
LAURA	I don't think that's true, Bill.
GEORGE	I haven't heard anything.

SUE   Bill, I think you're being very unreasonable.

             There is an awkward pause in which BILL and SUE
             lock eyes.

LAURA   (*to LILY and GEORGE*)   Well, it s a lovely night out
             there. Why don't the three of us go for a walk?

BILL   No.

SUE   You stay and finish up that wonderful looking
             chocolate paté, Laura, I'm sure you spent a lot of
             time on it. I'll just get Bill's coat and we'll go on
             home.

BILL   There is... somebody else, Sue. And I will be going
             home with her.

GEORGE   I think we've all had a little too much to drink,
             why don't we just...

SUE   Don't worry guys this isn't real. He's just drunk
             he's just trying to scare me because we had this
             argument about the new sofa – Come on honey,
             let's go home. Who is it. Who is it, Bill? She's not
             here, is she? You didn't, you didn't bring her to
             my neighbours', OUR friends' dinner party, to
             which I was invited. Laura! Laura for God's sake.

LILY   It's me.

             SUE laughs.

             Why do you think I'm joking?

             SUE looks at LILY, then looks at BILL.

             Bill??

BILL   This is – Lily.

LILY   How do you do, Susan?

SUE   Don't you call me by my name you FAT!! Please, I don't think you know what you're doing. This is not just me, this is a family, a family, we have two children.

LILY   I'm sorry.

SUE   Bill you are not leaving your children.

BILL   Sue, please.

SUE   YOU TOOK A VOW! In a CHURCH in front of a priest and my mother and your mother and your father and you swore to LOVE and honour and cherish till DEATH US DO PART till DEATH US DO PART BILL, it's your WORD your WORD.

BILL   I am breaking my word.

SUE   No!

BILL   YOU turned your back on me!! You you—look at you in that... sweatsuit thing you're not—I mean look at her, really, you're you're you're a kind of ... cartoon now, a... cartoon mum a... with your day-care meetings and neighbourhood fairs, you know what I mean Laura! Your face is a drawing your body, lines. The only time, the only time you are alive, electric again is... when you talk on the phone, to the other mums, there's a flush in your face, excitement, something rushing through your body, you laugh, loudly, you make all those won-derful female noises, you cry, your voice, like... music, or in the park, with Timmy and John, while they cavort with the other children at the drinking fountain, spraying the water and you talking and talking with all the mothers, storming, storming together your words like crazy swallows, swoop-ing and pivots and... landing... softly on a branch, a husband, one of us husbands walk in and it's like walking into... a large group of...

LILY	You see, I love... his body, Sue. I mean, I really love it. I love to suck it. I love to kiss it his body is my God, okay? His body–

SUE slaps LILY twice.

SUE	YOU... DON'T LIVE ON THIS STREET. You don't belong in this neighbourhood.

LILY contains herself from slapping SUE back.

Where did you meet this... woman? On the street?

BILL starts to try to answer.

In a house of prostitution? I demand to know–

LILY	I fucked him on the telephone, Susan, many many times.
SUE	That is a disgusting... lie.
LILY	Come on Suzy, don't you remember? You caught him a couple of times, on the downstairs phone with his pyjamas around his ankles, he told me!
SUE	(*the wind totally out of her*) I thought he was making... obscene phone calls.
BILL	Hello.
LILY	Hi there.
BILL	You got back to me quickly.
LILY	Fucking right.
BILL	Fucking right.
LILY	Your voice makes me crazy.
BILL	My voice.
LILY	I'm wet, Bill, wet just from hearing your voice.

BILL	What are you wearing?
LILY	Black silk underwear, red spiked heels, black lace bra.
BILL	Yeah? And what do you want? What do you want?
LILY	I want to suck your big cock, Bill, would you like me to do that? Would you like me to suck your big cock?
BILL	Oh baby, baby.
LILY	And then I want you to fuck me from behind all night long, can you do that? Can you do that for me, Bill?
BILL	Yes, yes, oh yes! Yes! Yes!
LILY	Oh, Bill!
SUE	BILLLLLLLLLLLLLLLLLLLLLLL!!!!!!! (*she physically attacks LILY*) Aghhhh! Listen, you, if you take my husband away from me and my children I will... kill you, I will I will... come when you are sleeping and I will pull your filthy tongue out of your filthy mouth. And then I will... feed it to our cat.
BILL	Susan.
SUE	(*forced laugh*) I didn't mean that, I really didn't. I'm sorry everybody, this is all just so ridiculous and embarrassing and I'm sure we'll all laugh about it someday I KNOW we will, but um... Bill? Won't you just... give me a chance? To show you? That I can? Be sexy? Cause I can, you know, much much more so than THAT creepy shit... don't you remember? Don't you remember before we were married how you loved to watch me dance? Come on, you did! Remember remember that wedding, Kevin and Leslie's? I wore that peach silk that you loved so much that dress drove you crazy! And after after the wedding we

were in that room in the Ramada Inn over the
water and I danced? You lay on the bed and you
just... watched me you loved it I... whooshed
whooshed in that dress, back and forth to this
thing on the radio back and oooh and back and
you were laughing and and (*laughs*) and whoosh.

> *Music beats louder, filling the room, and SUE
> begins a slow striptease.*

And whoosh... and... close to you, you're hard...
and far away and... turn... and whooosh... and...
let... my... hair... down... you – love my hair
whoosh and... zipppper... whoooo down so
slowwwww turn and turn... you watching lying
on the bed and ease... off my shoulders you love
my shoulders, elegant ohhh Billy, and down. Over
my body the soft silky down and
whoooooooooooooooo whooOOOOOOOO Billy.
Take me home, Billy, take me home and let's make
mad passionate love! Please.

> *BILL and LILY leave. GEORGE and LAURA pick
> up SUE's clothing and bring it to her. LAURA
> dresses her.*

LAURA   Honey, I'm sorry.

SUE   Aghh don't feel sorry for me it's fine, everything
will be fine because... his colon cancer's gonna
come back, don't you think? Dr. Neville said he
had a sixty-forty chance, it will. And she'll drop
him, for sure, don't you think? And he will let me
nurse him I will... feed him broth, with a spoon,
like I did my mum, and I will hold, I will hold his
sweet head in my chest till till his lips are black
and his eyes... like bright dead stars and he is
dead and I will stay I will stay with his body, in
the hospital room because I did love that body...
oh I did *love—that—body* once.

ISOBEL   Susan, Susan, Susan. The boy with the arrow ha
killed you, ha? Where's your helper now? Oh
Susan, you can't help me now you can't take me
home. (*to the audience*) Hey! Who gonna take me

home? You? You gotta car? What kinda car you got? Trans-Am? What about bus tickets? You gotta bus tickets? C'mon. Come on. COME ON. SOMEBODY. What I'm sposed to do, ha? Who gonna take me home? Who gonna take me home?

> *ISOBEL finds a watching place. A few hours later, at LAURA and GEORGE's, LAURA clears the table.*

LAURA   Poor Suzy. Poor poor Suzy.

GEORGE   (*half asleep*) Yeahh. Chee.

LAURA   God, that is the worst thing I have ever seen happen to anybody.

> *GEORGE and LAURA laugh hysterically and imitate SUE in the previous scene.*

GEORGE   Whoosh! That peach silk, oh baby take me home.

LAURA   Take me home, Bill. Let's make mad passionate love. (*stops imitating SUE*) I don't know, I mean I know she needs a friend badly, I am her friend I mean I love her. George, how can you laugh? This is important. If she calls me tomorrow, what should I say? I'm just going to say, I'm going to say, "SUZY? I feel really badly for you and I think you're a wonderful person but you will have to look somewhere else for–"

GEORGE   Nice.

LAURA   GEORGE, you KNOW–

GEORGE   You always say she's your best friend, Laura, "my BEST–"

LAURA   She is! But George, are you forgetting Maria? I had a nervous breakdown because of that woman and her problem how could you FORGET?

GEORGE   I was on the book tour, Loo.

LAURA   I told you about it a hundred times, how could you forget?

GEORGE   I was on the book tour – Loo.

LAURA   George, you are so insensitive, I can't believe this. I told you about it one hundred times. How can you forget?

> *GEORGE grabs a tablecloth and wraps it around his head, like a shawl, speaking in a Portuguese accent.*

GEORGE   How could I forget, how could I forget?

LAURA   George.

GEORGE   Looka this. Me? I donta forget nothing.

LAURA   George I'm going to bed, Molly gets up in two hours and it's always me that gets up with her of course.

> *She walks around the circle.*

GEORGE/
MARIA   LAURA.

> *Now he speaks as MARIA, ISOBEL'S mother. ISOBEL recognizes her.*

LAURA   George! Come to bed.

GEORGE/
MARIA   LAURA.

LAURA   Maria.

MARIA   I am... so sorry to be coming to your house, maybe you busy, I don't know–

LAURA   No, no, please come in Maria, I'm just – reading the paper the kids are at school and–

MARIA starts shaking violently and keening. She looks like she is in shock.

Maria?... uh... Maria? Are you alright? You look – why don't you sit down. Here. Sit down. Can I get you a drink of water?

MARIA starts to keen with grief, quite quietly.

MARIA   Eeeeeeee

LAURA   Maria? Maria... are you alright? Maria, Maria please tell me... what's...

MARIA   ...I think... I think... Antonio–

LAURA   Your husband? Something happened to your husband?

MARIA continues to keen.

It's okay, Maria, you don't have to tell me if you don't–

MARIA   Five o'clock in the morning I cook: smelt and three scramble eggs, nice bread, coffee. For Antony must work long day, construction on highway, long day in the sun, he come from his shower to kitchen, but he don't want. He gotta rat in his stomach that day he say, make a joke, don't want my cooking eat a little bitta bread and just small glass of milk and he go, catch his subway. I fold. I fold clothes one pile for Antony, one pile for me, one for Maria, Romeo, ISOBEL and Luig, my hands fold the clothes but my... (*gesture indicating self or soul*)

LAURA   Sure, you go on automatic – I–

MARIA   Like I fold myself too, and I go in his body, maybe, you know, his... hand to, wipe off his face when he hot and too sweat I am there;

She walks operatically down-stage and delivers the rest of the speech, which should be like an aria.

I am foldin a light sheet of blue then and sudden, I can see through his eye, am at subway, in him, he stands on the platform, is empty, empty and I am his head, circles and circles like red birds flying around and around I am his throat, tight, cannot breathe enough air in my body the floor the floor move, and sink in, rise up rise like a wall like a killin wave turn turn me in circles with teeth in circles and under and over I fall!

ISOBEL falls on an imaginary track in front of her mother.

I fall on the silver track nobody move I hearing the sound. The sound of the rats in the tunnel their breath like a basement these dark rats running running towards me I am stone I am earth cannot scream cannot move the rats tramp... trample my body flat-ten and every bone splinter like...

We hear the sound of a strong wind as the "Sugar Meeting" is being set up on the stage. By the end of the wind, LAURA is at her table, addressing the meeting.

LAURA   Good evening everybody.

GEORGE   Good evening.

RON   Hi Laura.

LAURA   I uh might as well get straight down to business. As head and sole member of the menu research committee, I have spent some three weeks doing... a great deal... of... research, and even a little detective work...

RON and GEORGE are talking to one another.

...and I would like to make my presentation tonight without too much interruption, thank you.

GEORGE   Go for it.

RON   No problem.

LAURA   POINT ONE. Sugar: I strongly recommend that
we make a concerted effort to eradicate all sugar
from the children's diet. Sugar is an overstimu-
lant, sugar is empty calories, sugar rots...

RON   Uh, I have to say, that, while I agree, sure, too
much sugar is not a good thing, that once in a
while...

LAURA   Would you let your four-year-old smoke "once in
a while"?

                 A murmur from the crowd.

RON   (*with a little laugh*) I don't really think you can
equate...

                 ISOBEL rises and walks into the meeting.

LAURA   Sugar is a known carcinogen, Ron, I have a study
right here...

JILL   Lettuce is a known carcinogen, for God's sake!

ISOBEL   Hey! Boys! Girls! Looka this! I think tha they
can't see me! They no see Isobel! Wha happen?
Wha happen?

JILL   Okay as chairperson, I say – let's cut the comments
and raise our hands for questions. Laura? You
want to go ahead?

LAURA   Yes, thank you, Jill. Uh. (*clears her throat*) It has
come to my attention...

                 GEORGE groans.

                 Excuse me, I have to ask you why you groaned
like that, George, did I say something wrong?

JILL	George, penalty for groaning out of turn, just kidding.
GEORGE	No, no, I'm sorry, I just, I don't know, I just... have a kind of a hard time with "meeting... talk"... "it has come to my attention."
LAURA	Well, I'm very sorry, George, if you have a better way of–
JILL	That was uncalled for George, really.
RON	George, your mother's calling you.
	General laughter.
JILL	Let's let Laura continue please, so we can get out of here...
ISOBEL	I think I invisible!
LAURA	Thank you Jill. I have NOTICED, if you don't like "it has come to my attention," I have noticed that in this nursery school they are... subtly, and I'm sure unwittingly, encouraging an addiction to sugar in our children.
RHONDA	Hey, that's not true.
LAURA	Rhonda, I'm SAYING it's not intentional...
RHONDA	The kids are not...
LAURA	PLEASE LET ME TALK.
JILL	Go ahead, Laura, please.
LAURA	I have noticed that sugar is used as a reward. If you're good we'll make cookies tomorrow. If you tidy up you get chocolate cake as a reward. You are creating... unwittingly, I concede, you are creating TOMORROW'S COKE ADDICTS... TO–
RHONDA	EXCUSE ME I HAVE TO SAY THAT, AS THE CAREGIVER, I RESENT THIS.

LAURA	Rhonda, I'm not accusing just you, I think you are fabulous with the kids, it's our whole society...
RHONDA	I am not creating drug addicts.
JILL	Rhonda, Laura does not mean any of this personally, I think that's...
LAURA	I'm saying it's a small step from sugar addiction to–
RON	Excuse me, I have to say, all food is sugar...
LAURA	REFINED SUGAR IS FAST-ACTING, RON, IT BURDENS THE PANCREAS.
GEORGE	I think you are taking this a little too seriously, Laura, we're just talking about a few cookies now and then for heaven's sake.
LAURA	WE ARE TALKING ABOUT A LIFETIME ADDICTION AND I DON'T THINK IT SHOULD BE TAKEN LIGHTLY.
JILL	Laura, are you willing to listen to a response from Rhonda?
LAURA	Sure.
RHONDA	I would just... like to say that I, also have done... a great deal of studying diet and menu and that, and I fully agree with Laura that sugar is... something to be avoided, IF YOU CAN. Listen, if I'm giving the kids yoghurt, they won't eat it without honey they won't, so I figure, a bit of honey is worth getting the yoghurt down em...
LAURA	BULLSHIT THAT IS ABSOLUTE UNADULTERATED BULLSHIT.
RHONDA	I beg your pardon, Laura?
LAURA	You don't know what you're saying, Rhonda.

RHONDA   If you don't trust me, Laura...

LAURA   Rhonda...

RHONDA   I do not encourage sugar, I do not hold it up as a reward, ever, I have never done that.

LAURA   You re lying, Rhonda.

RON   WAIT A MINUTE HOLD ON JUST A...

LAURA   SHUT UP RON. LISTEN. LISTEN TO ME RHONDA. I FOUND OUT THAT JUST LAST FRIDAY, LAST FRIDAY, AS A REWARD, YOU TOOK SIX KIDS, INCLUDING MY TWINS, TO A DOUGHNUT SHOP. YOU TOOK THEM TO A DOUGHNUT SHOP AND BOUGHT THEM EACH A JELLY DOUGHNUT.
I think I screamed for five minutes when the twins told me that I just couldn't believe it they started harassing me every five minutes, "Mum, if we're good, can we have a jelly doughnut?" I don't think they'd ever HEARD OF JELLY DOUGH-NUTS BEFORE THAT!! I find it unconscionable, UNCONSCIONABLE that a jelly doughnut would be the sole purpose of an excursion.

RHONDA   Um, I can explain that. It was a Friday, right, and I happen to get severe cramps with my period, right? And I was very sick that day and the kids had bad bad cabin fever, well...

LAURA   (*overlapping*) And the Friday before that it was popsicles, Rhonda, I'm not blaming you I'm say-ing you need to be re-educated, we all do, smelling the flowers is a reason to go for a walk, not getting a poisonous body-destroying drug...

RHONDA   LET MEEEEE TALLLLLK. LET ME TALK LET ME TALLLLLLLLLLLK!! I feel... nailed to the wall by you lady, nailed right to the fucking wall. I have to say and something else I have to say is that I think you are... are very... inconsiderate... of

feelings! I brought up two kids on what I feed
your kids, and they turned out just fine, are you
telling me what I feed my kids isn't good enough
for your kids? You know the funny thing is,
Laura, you may be a bitch on wheels, but lookin at
all the rest of you, Laura? at least you're honest
you are. Youse others, what you're thinkin is... it
really doesn't matter what they get at the day care
the real learning is at home, that's where youse
teach your kids to become – huh. Here I am saying "youse" I haven't said that since I was a kid!
that's how flustered I am – at home you teach
your kids... to be... higher kind of people, higher
kind of people don't eat Kraft slices and tuna
casserole, I've seen that kinda laugh in your voic-
es, all of you, when you say, "Oh, they had *tuna
casserole*," I seen, I have seen the roll in your eyes
at the grace before meals, or the tidy-up song, or
the stars we give out for citizen of the week, you
think, oh well the kid is happy, well cared for, we
can undo all that and we can make the kids high
people like ourselves better people, more better
people than the poor little teacher who reads
ROMANCE, yes, yes, JILL MATHINS, I saw you
showin my book, my novel to RON there and
Cathy and havin a big giggle, you think I didn't
see that? You think the books you read are deeper
more... higher, well it's the same story, don't you
see that? What's makin me cry in my book is,
when ya come right down to it, is exactly the same
thing that's makin you cry in your book, oh yes,
oh yes and I'll tell you something, I'll tell all of
you I GREW UP ON THAT. I grew up on jelly
doughnuts and butter tarts, and chocolate ice-
cream, and I happen to think they're a wonderful
thing. I happen to agree with the mice and the
cockroaches and the horses and birds that treats
are a wonderful thing, you need treats, you need
treats in this life, each bit of a treat can wipe out a
nasty word, every bite of a jelly doughnut cleans
out your soul it is a gift from GOD, a wonderful
gift from GOD and I for one... I for one... I... for...
your eyes, eh? Your eyes are all the same colour
and shape like a picture, a... freaky art picture all
the same in a row like dark soldiers raisin your...

ISOBEL shoots everybody there except RHONDA with her finger. There are real shot sounds although ISOBEL is imagining this.

ISOBEL   (*big laugh, then struts*) Rho-HONDA! Bebbe! Beautiful belle! I have killed those dirty bastards, babe, I have killed them dirty dead. I am your harmy, Rhohonda! And you! You gonna take me home!

ISOBEL falls and wraps herself around RHONDA's feet. Music. A restaurant. DAVID takes his place behind the bar, another person is sitting alone at a table. RHONDA and her friend JOANNE meet for drinks. They are laughing. ISOBEL watches.

RHONDA   Oh man is this Singapore Sling fantastic.

JOANNE   My Fuzzy Navel is warm. Hot!

RHONDA   SEND it back! We're paying through the teeth for these drinks. Waiter, take this thing back!

JOANNE   No, I like it this way, honest, Rhonda, I do.

DAVID   Is there a problem with your cocktail?

JOANNE   No no no no please...

DAVID   I could take it back–

JOANNE   No.

RHONDA   Are you sure?

JOANNE   I'm sure.

DAVID   Okaaay.

RHONDA   Ohhh Christ, I'd like to just sit and drink all afternoon to tell you the truth.

JOANNE   I thought you quit heavy drinkin.

RHONDA	I did. I'm just... down in the dumps.
JOANNE	Why, ya on your time?
ISOBEL	Is this my home? This is not my home!
RHONDA	No no no, I get happy then, no, it's just... work.
JOANNE	Yeah, Jeez I'm glad I'm not workin it made me crazy, what's goin on? the kids at the day care gettin to ya?
RHONDA	No no it's not the kids, the kids are great, it's the parents.
JOANNE	Uh oh. That same B-I-T-C-H?
RHONDA	No, she was quite good this time, strangely enough, it's another one.
JOANNE	They all look like bitches to me in their leather pants. Stuck up, puttin their kids in forty-five-dollar shoes, I looked at the price of them REEboks for kids – the other day when I picked you up I saw three of those kids had those shoes on I couldn't believe my eyes.
RHONDA	Yeah, well, they're pretty well-off, but I don't hold that against them, I mean, who wouldn't be if they had the chance, right?
JOANNE	Well that's a good point SO...
RHONDA	We had this meeting, okay?
JOANNE	RHONDA. Excuse me!
RHONDA	What?
JOANNE	(*intake of breath*) ...I don't know.
RHONDA	What do you mean?

JOANNE	I mean... no, I don't know.
RHONDA	Joanne.
JOANNE	I mean... oh God, I wasn't going to tell nobody–
RHONDA	You're pregnant again?
JOANNE	No no no no, if only, I...
RHONDA	JOANNE, I'M YOUR BEST FRIEND.
JOANNE	YOU'RE MY BEST FRIEND?
RHONDA	Yes, you know that!
JOANNE	THEN SWEAR ON YOUR MOTHER'S LIFE.
RHONDA	What?
JOANNE	That you will do what I'm gonna ask you.
RHONDA	Joanne, what is this?
JOANNE	Just... swear.
RHONDA	I'm not swearing on my mother's life without knowing what it is, she's got enough problems...
JOANNE	Okay, your husband s life.
RHONDA	Okay, I swear on the asshole's life. There. Now what?
JOANNE	You remember... I had this pain in my back?
RHONDA	Yeah, for the last few months, every time ya bend down.
JOANNE	SEARING pain, every time I moved...
RHONDA	...Okay...

JOANNE	Well remember I told you I went to that specialist and he said he was gonna do some tests?
RHONDA	Right, uh-huh.
JOANNE	Well–
RHONDA	You gotta go in and have an operation and you want me to take your kids, no problem of COURSE I'll take them Jo, for God's–
JOANNE	(*overlapping*) No. No, I mean, you might have to take the kids but that's only... part of it.
RHONDA	Joanne, I really don't like guessing games.
JOANNE	Shadows... that's what they call them, and... it is... the very worst thing it could be, and the... kind, the kind is of the bone.
RHONDA	Oh boy.
JOANNE	Yeah.
RHONDA	(*whispers*) Jo...
JOANNE	Don't... don't touch me. I'll go hysterical please.
RHONDA	YOU... want a cigarette?
JOANNE	Yeah.

RHONDA lights one and gives it to her.

Ya know, I have to go to the bathroom, like, real bad but I'm not gonna go, ya know why? Cause every time... I sit down to pee I feel my whole life drainin out of me, just draining out with the pee, goin... outa me, into the water down in the pipes, and under the... friggin... GROUND. That's where I'll be, Rho, that's where I'm gonna... (*fights to regain her composure*) I'll come home with the groceries? Like after dark? and I'll see Frank and the kids through the window, in the livin-room, right?

Watchin TV, or drawing on paper, cuttin out stuff, whatever, and I'll stand on the porch and watch em, just... playing... on the floor, and I think... that's life, that's life goin on without me, it'll be just like that, only I won't be here with the groceries, I'll be under the ground under the ground with my flesh fallin off a my face and I just can't take it. You know in that picture? That picture I had in my bedroom growing up?

RHONDA   UHH–

JOANNE   My aunt and uncle sent me that from England, the poster it's OPHELIA, from this play by Shakespeare, right? And she she – got all these flowers, tropical flowers, wild flowers, white roses, violets and buttercups, everything she loved and she kinda weaved them all together. Then she got the heaviest dress she could find... you know how dresses in the olden days were so long and heavy, with petticoats and that? And she got this heavy heavy blue dress, real... blue and then she wrapped all these pretty pretty flowers round and round her body, round her head, and her hair, she had this golden, wavy hair, long, and then she steps down the bank, and she lies, on her back, in the stream. She lies there, but the stream runs so fast she's on her back and she goes. It pulls her along so fast and she's lookin at the sky and the clouds, and she's singing little songs "I'm lookin over a four-leaf clover" – and being pulled so fast by a clear cold water pulled along and she's not scared, she's not scared at all, she's calm, so happy! And just ever so slowly her dress, gets heavier, right? Then, then, she gets caught on a stick, like a branch, of a willow tree, and her dress pulls her down, soft, she's still singin down deep deep deep to the bottom of the stream and with all these "fantastic garlands," these beautiful flowers all around her—"one's for the roses that blew down the lane"—she dies, Rhon, she dies... good. She dies good.

RHONDA   That's... something.

JOANNE   I want to die like that. But... I don't... want to do it all alone, I mean, I want you to help me, with the flowers, and with the dress, and my hair, I want you to make sure the willow branch is there, and the stream is right, and maybe... maybe that... Frank... sees I... wouldn't mind him seein... me in that stream, with the flowers, and the heavy blue dress... I wouldn't mind if you took maybe some pictures of me like that and then you could have them printed and given out at the funeral, something like that... just, you know, two by four, colour, whatever, it's the one thing that would make it alright – it's the one thing...

RHONDA   I just... I don't know, Jo, you know I'd do anything to make it alright...

JOANNE   Well this is what I want, Rhonda, it's really really really what I want. Are you going to help me?

RHONDA   I uh – think you need to see a counsellor, Jo, you know they have counsellors that... specialize in these... situations I'm surprised your doctor didn't...

JOANNE   You think I m crazy.

RHONDA   No no, Joanne, I just think that... your situation is so hard that you are not quite yourself, I mean this is not... you, the Joanne I know is practical she... you should believe in the treatments, Jo, they do work sometimes, they really do, and the Joanne I know-would never ask a friend to help... her... is one of the most thoughtful people that I know, of other people and how the hell, how the hell do you think that I could live with that after, eh?? I mean it's all very lovely and that, your picture, in your room but that's a picture, that's a picture, you dimwit! The real of it would be awful, the stalks of the flowers would be chokin you, and the smells of them would make you sick, all those smells comin at you when you're feelin so sick to begin with, and the stream, well if you're talking about the Humber River or any stream in this

country you're talkin filth, in the Humber River
you're even talkin sewage, Jo, you're talkin ciga-
rette packages and used condoms and old tam-
pons floating by you're talking freezin, you'd start
shakin from head to toe you're talkin rocks gashin
your head you're talkin a bunch of longhairs and
goofs on the banks yellin at you callin you whore-
bag sayin what they'd like to do to you, you're
talkin... and where would you get a dress like that,
eh? You'd never find the one in the picture, Jo,
it'd be too tight at the neck and the waist, it'd be a
kind of material that itches your skin, even worse
wet, drives you nut-crazy, the blue would be off,
wouldn't look right your shoes wouldn't match
you could never find the same colour, Joanne. You
can't become a picture, do you know what I
mean? I mean you can't... BE... a picture, okay?

*They freeze. ISOBEL runs from her watching place,
around the circle screaming; she has realized, listen-
ing to JOANNE, that she is not lost, but dead, mur-
dered seventeen years before.*

ISOBEL   AAHHHHHHHHHHHH!! I am dead!
I have been bones for seventeen years, missing,
missing, my face in the TV and newspapers,
posters, everybody lookin for, nobody find, I am
gone, I am dead, I AM DEADLY DEAD! Down! It
was night, was a lion, roar!! with red eyes: he
come closer (*silent scream*) come closer (*silent
scream*) ROAR tear my throat out ROAR tear my
eyes out... ROAR I am kill! I am kill! I am no
more!

Music.

(*to JOANNE*) We are both pictures now. WHO
WILL TAKE US? WHO WILL TAKE US TO
HEAVEN, HA?

*Lights down. Cathedral bells ring. DAVID is out-
side, walking down the street.*

DAVID   God, that customer dying of bone cancer. I didn't
                 even want to touch her glass. I don't know she
                 had that look, that dead look. I mean I almost felt
                 hostile.

ISOBEL   (*inside the cathedral*) I WANT TO GO TO HEAVEN
                 NOW!

                 *She sees a life-size statue of the Virgin Mary and
                 approaches it.*

                 Holy Mary Mother of God. Will you take Isobel to
                 heaven now, please?

                 *She lies at the base of the statue, her hand touching
                 the statue's foot.*

DAVID   God that cathedral is beautiful, funny, I've passed
                 it every day on my way out from work and I've
                 never really looked at it. Look at the stonework,
                 those *spires*–

                 *He opens the church doors and enters. The doors
                 slam behind him.*

                 Oh I love this it's so... the air is s ... holy it IS, look
                 at those bird-bath things full of holy water, I love
                 it it's so primitive. (*he splashes some on his face*) In
                 the name of the Father... the Son, and the Holy–

FATHER
HAYES   Good evening.

                 DAVID shrieks, startled. His shriek echoes.

                 It's alright, it's alright. Have you come for...

DAVID   Confession. I've come for confession, 8:30, yes?
                 I'm not too late, am I, see, I just finished work,
                 and...

FATHER
HAYES   Not too late, of course not.

FATHER HAYES goes into his part of the confessional.

DAVID   (*to himself*) I guess just – God I don't remember a THING about what to do!!

We hear the wooden barrier being opened, and the priest begins the Latin prayer.

FATHER HAYES   In the name of the Father, and the Son, and the Holy Spirit.

DAVID   (*overlapping*) Oh God he's saying something–

FATHER HAYES   May the Lord be in your heart and help you to confess your sins with true sorrow. Let us listen to the Lord as he speaks to us: I will give them a new heart and put a new spirit within them; I will remove the strong heart from their bodies and replace it with a natural heart, so that they will live according to my statutes, and observe and carry out my ordinances; thus they shall be my people and I will be their God.

DAVID   (*overlapping*) I think it's Latin, isn't that against Papal Law? I should report him to the Vatican and have him defrocked here goes nothing–

FATHER HAYES finishes the prayer.

AHH – FORGIVE ME FATHER FOR I have sinned. It has been... four weeks since my last confession. These are my sins?... OKAY, told Barb I'd be there last night for dinner with her and the niece and nephew – didn't show up didn't phone nothing, was in a mad PASH with my hockey player. I was very cruel to Daniel Thursday, saw him at Billy's – the club? And I don't know, the way he was looking at me drove me CRAZY CRAZY he was mooning! Well I walked up to him and told him to "quit mooning I'd rather see your hairy ass than that pathetic face, face it!"

I said, "Face it you old fag, you have been
dumped, DUMPED!" That was really mean, that's
gotta be more than a venial sin, AND THEN, then,
yesterday, I walked through a park? And I saw a
large group of poor children playing, and I just
thought they were trouble; I wondered why God
had put them in the world, really, isn't that
unkind? THEN today I saw a fat lady eating an
ice-cream cone and I said, I think quite audibly I
said "disgusting" oh AND I did not stand up in
the subway the incredibly packed subway, for a
hugely pregnant lady and her kid, I just didn't feel
like it. Quite the catalogue, eh? Oh and another
thing, I've lied to you already. I haven't been to
confession in fifteen years, haven't stepped in a
church in fifteen years, just... did it on a whim,
don't ask me why I was passing by on my way...

**FATHER
HAYES**   AND you felt the hand of GOD?

DAVID   Well... it was just a whim – really...

**FATHER
HAYES**   David.

DAVID   How do you know my name?

**FATHER
HAYES**   David I know your name better than I know my
own.

DAVID   Wait a minute, wait a minute, I think maybe this is
some odd coincidence because although my name
is DAVID, I don't actually know you at all, so...

**FATHER
HAYES**   There's nothing odd about it, David, you were an
altar boy for me, two years, for two years you
served, in 1957 and 1958 at St. Bernard's in
Moncton, New Brunswick. Remember?

DAVID   Moncton? We were around there for a couple of
years–

FATHER HAYES   You were a believer, David, the other boys were just forced into it by their parents, you believed in every statue every–

DAVID   Father Hayes? You – are Father Hayes?

FATHER HAYES   I am.

DAVID   You're still alive?

FATHER HAYES   I think.

DAVID   But you were so old even way back then!

FATHER HAYES   Not really.

DAVID   I remember you now. I remember you did look old, because you stooped, and you had white hair already didn't you?

FATHER HAYES   Indeed, I was prematurely white...

DAVID   White hair and... and... red eyes.

FATHER HAYES   I... suffered from allergies, hay fever. I'm sorry if it frightened you.

DAVID   I guess maybe it did frighten me a bit, Father, but you know how young boys are–

FATHER HAYES   I am sorry, but, but...

DAVID   No no, I... look, I uh–

FATHER HAYES   David, I want...

DAVID	...don't mean to be impolite but I'd like you to be honest with me, sort of man to man I... I always got the impression that you were looking at me much more than you looked at the other boys am I right?
FATHER HAYES	Well...
DAVID	I felt... I felt as though your eyes were devouring me.
FATHER HAYES	No, no, no...
DAVID	No?? I'm gay, Father, you can be honest with me. I'll forgive you, I mean you never actually did anything, you never even touched me, you just... looked. You kept looking at me – tell me, tell me the truth.
FATHER HAYES	It was not what you think, no, no please–
DAVID	Confess to me Father, come on, come on...
FATHER HAYES	I make my confessions on a regular...
DAVID	Have you confessed this sin?
FATHER HAYES	No, no I haven't, but–
DAVID	God loves sinners who confess, Father, you taught me that, as long as you speak up and you're sorry as hell, you're okay, you still got your ticket to heaven, but you won't you won't Father, if you don't tell me, you'll wither in LIMBO! I suffered, I need you to tell me! CONFESS...
FATHER HAYES	I'm due to a christening. I have to shave first, there's a big party, I–

DAVID	You would christen a baby with this sin, bobbing on the surface, bobbing? Confess, you son of a bitch. Con–
FATHER HAYES	Forgive me Father for I have sinned.
DAVID	Alright.
FATHER HAYES	I looked at you, David, because... I... because... I wanted... to... remember... you.
DAVID	Remember me?
FATHER HAYES	Because... of what was to happen, in the water: oh OH when the day arrived, when the picnic came round, in July, that Canada Day picnic? I had a bad feeling, I had... a very bad feeling indeed. We all piled out of the cars: families, priests, nuns, altar boys, piled out and lugged all those picnic baskets to tables under trees. The grownups all fussed with food and drink while the kids, all of you children, ran ran in your white bare feet to the water, throwing stones and balls, and a warning sound a terrible, the sound of deep nausea filled my ears and I looked up and saw you, dancing on the water, and I saw a red circle, a red, almost electric circle, dazzling round and round like waves, spinning round your head and body. I thought watch, watch that boy, on this day he will surely drown, he *will*. David, *I knew that you would die.* And all because of the chicken. The twenty-nine-pound chicken brought there by Mrs. Henry grown on her brother's farm, everyone had talked and talked about that chicken, who would carve that chicken, Mrs. Henry took it out you skipped along the shore, she laid it on the table, "FATHER HAYES, YOU GO AHEAD AND CARVE, AND DON'T MAKE A MESS OF IT OR YOU WON'T SEE ME AT MASS NEXT SUNDAY." Everyone laughed laughed the men, the men drinking beer, watching me, sure they're thinking, "Watch him

carve like a woman," most men hate priests, you
know this is a fact, I could see them thinking cruel
thoughts under hooded eyes and practised grins;
my sin was the sin of pride! The sin of pride
David, I started to carve, didn't want to look up,
lest I wreck the bird. You see at that moment that
chicken was worth more, indeed worth more...
than your LIFE, David I SHUT OUT the warning
voice and I – carved. I carved and carved and ran
into trouble, real trouble I remember thinking,
"Damn how does any person do it, it's a terrible
job," people behave as if it's nothing, but it's terrible, I kept at it, I wouldn't give up, I wouldn't
look up till I'd finished, and I finished carving,
and I had made a massacre. The men turned
away the women... murmured comfort, and before
I looked up I had a hope, a hard hope, that you
were still skipping on the rocks and shouting
insults to your pals all hands reached for chicken
and bread, potato salad, chocolate cake I looked I
looked up and your hand from the sea, your hand,
far away, was reaching, reaching for me far away...
oh no! I ran, and tripped, fell on my face ran
again, I could not speak ran to the water and
shouted as loud as I could but my voice was so
tiny; I saw your hand, ran to the fisherman close,
he wasn't home his fat daughter and I, in the skiff,
not enough wind no wind, paddling paddling,
you a small spot nothing then nothing the sun
burns our faces our red red faces.

DAVID And I... was... never found?

**FATHER
HAYES** And now... you have come!! You have finally
come!!

DAVID And what have I come for?

FATHER HAYES is sleeping.

DAVID Uh... Father? Uh-listen... I'm sorry. I'm sorry but I
never died. You got the wrong guy I knew you...
some other time – I mean, shit, I wish I had died, I
only wish, it would have made my life so much

more interesting... I grew up, I grew up. Listen if I had drowned in the sea, in Moncton, New Brunswick a beautiful perfect young boy, if I was... pulled by the sea if I reached and was lost, and all those people felt this loss, a loss all their lives, mother father brothers and sister friends a dark ache, somewhere in their chest for what could have been, they could all imagine, you see, what could have been Father Father? I forgive you, I forgive you Father, it was nice on the water, you know? It was neat, so calm, as I slipped underneath I wasn't scared, I'll tell ya. I wasn't scared a bit. The water was so... nice!!

Music. ISOBEL dances joined by the cast one by one until they are all dancing fully. Cast dance off one by one leaving ISOBEL, who freezes. Blackout.

ACT II

Sounds of kids playing in a park, a group of mothers chat. ISOBEL watches.

CHRISTINE   How's your pregnancy going, dear?

Lion roar.

ISOBEL   I hear the LION, I hear the Lion ROAR!!

ELLEN   Wonderful! I finally feel... good for something. LEO, SHARE IT. Share it please.

CHRISTINE   Not me NOT me when I was pregnant I felt as useful as a cow. A large, stupid...

ELLEN   Christine!!

CHRISTINE   EMMA! Five more minutes honey! Mummy's got to go to work! Well, considering I despised the man whose child I was carrying–

ELLEN   I suppose that would... alter things – GOOD CATCH, Leo!

SUE   Hi guys. Timmy, just five minutes. Remember, your father's coming to get you at five.

CHRISTINE   Sue, I love that blouse! Really suits you!

ELLEN   Gorgeous!

SUE   Thank you, I'm organizing a bake sale, if you can believe it, for the community centre over on Ash Street. PLEASE say you'll bake, or sell tickets, even a promise to buy–

ISOBEL   I must tell these peoples, I must tell them now!

ELLEN   Forget me, I'm a diabetic! I can't even look at the stuff.

SUE   Tim! Why don't you try the swing? You love swings.

CHRISTINE   Okay, put me down for fudge brownies, if my kids don't eat them first.

> *GEORGE enters with a kid's bicycle.*

George! How's the book going?

GEORGE   Well, well, very well indeed!! And how's the busiest freelancer in town? Bradley, don't push so hard!

CHRISTINE   Overworked and underpaid.

GEORGE   What else is new?

> *RON enters.*

Ron! Why aren't you at your office?

ELLEN   We're telling!

GEORGE   Good. Bradley!

SUE   Tim? Why don't you try the swing?

CHRISTINE   RON did you get my note? EMMA PUT IT BACK!

RON   Yes, I did, I – I – I–

ISOBEL   (*hitting them*) Shut up Boy! Shut up Girl! I say I say it's time!! He's in the streets get them out he's in the streets save your children take their hand take their leg.

SUE   Isobel! I saw this girl before, she–

ISOBEL   I say shut up! I say LISTEN TO ME NOW! Can you no hear? Listen! Can you nooo–

> *All freeze except SUE, who crosses slowly towards the children.*

SUE   Timmy?

ISOBEL   (*goes to her*) The lion is here, in your streets. He is
           trying to kill you, to kill all of your children. He
           really really is.

           *She picks up a great crooked stick which she will
           carry until she says "I love you" to BEN in the
           final scene.*

           Watch me! (*laughs*) I am your HARMY! (*laughs*) I
           am your SAINT! I am your HARMY! Watch me,
           watch me, (*a war cry*) I WILL KILL THE LION
           NOW!!

           *Thunderstorm as SUE shouts "TIMMMYY!!" and
           the others ad lib to their children, e.g., "Quick, you
           don't want to get wet!" All exit. A kid's bike is left
           on-stage. Blackout. Lights up on CHRISTINE
           walking towards SCARLETT'S basement apart-
           ment, "tracked" by ISOBEL.*

ISOBEL   This girl, Christine, Christine, this girl, SHE will
           take me to the lion, yes, for she... she is very hard.
           Harrrrd. HARRRRRRRD!!

CHRISTINE 116 Carlisle. Lord what a stench. What could that
           be? (*knocks*)

SCARLETT   Come in!

CHRISTINE Scarlett Deer?

SCARLETT   That's my name, don't wear it out, has to last a
           lifetime!!

CHRISTINE I'm Christine Pierce from the *Telegraph*. We talked
           on the phone.

SCARLETT   Have a seat.

CHRISTINE Thank you. Nice place.

SCARLETT   What, this hole? Sorry if it stinks, I cooked chick-
            en today an ever since I ate it I been fartin up a
            storm. Dead chicken farts, that's what my brother
            always said.

CHRISTINE   Scarlett, I don't have a lot of time, so is it all right
            if I ask you some questions?

SCARLETT   Sure, How does it feel to be an ugly geek? Fine
            thank you, fuck you very much.

CHRISTINE   Scarlett, advanced cerebral palsy is a serious hand-
            icap. Don't you feel that living on your own is
            dangerous?

SCARLETT   Would you like to live in a freakhouse?

CHRISTINE   Well, Scarlett, I–

SCARLETT   Freedom, freedom girl, I'd rather fuckin rot on the
            floor of my own home than be well-fed and cared
            for in a freakhouse.

CHRISTINE   What you're saying, then, is that above all things,
            you cherish freedom. That you would rather risk–

SCARLETT   Once when my volunteers were sick? All of em
            were sick, right? And I just wanted to see what
            the hell I would do? I lay in my own shit and piss
            for three days.

CHRISTINE   Good Lord, what–

SCARLETT   I coulda phoned somebody, my parents live down
            the street, but I just wanted to see... I wanted to
            see how long I'd survive, I wanted to see if I could
            do it.

CHRISTINE   Well, who did you eventually–

SCARLETT   My mother, my poor mother. And it makes me
            sick, sick, because what will I do when they die?
            They're old you know, they're gonna die soon.

CHRISTINE   What will you do?

SCARLETT   I'll die on the floor in my shit and piss.

CHRISTINE   Scarlett, do you have any hobbies; that is, what do you do between volunteers, do you have favourite soap operas or game shows, or–

SCARLETT   I screw my brains out.

CHRISTINE   (*a weak laugh*) No, seriously, Scarlett.

SCARLETT   You think I'm kiddin? You think I sit around and watch game shows and uh stare out the window waitin for the next volunteer? No way, girlie, I git it ONNN.

CHRISTINE   You're... sexually active, then?

SCARLETT   Shocked, aren't you, pretty pea?

CHRISTINE   No.

SCARLETT   YOU ARE TOO YOU LYING BITCH!!

CHRISTINE   Alright, I will admit, I am... surprised. I suppose the public perception of handicapped people is somewhat-skewered.

SCARLETT   You think you're bettern me, dontcha?

CHRISTINE   Oh Scarlett, really I...

SCARLETT   Well I'll tell you somethin, Christine, my boyfriend wouldn't rub your tittie. And you think he's handicapped? No way, babe, I'm not fucking a freak.

CHRISTINE   Well, I'm very happy for you, really Scarlett.

SCARLETT   Bullshit, you think it's sick.

CHRISTINE   No, honestly Scarlett, I don't! I think everybody deserves to have a happy sex life.

SCARLETT   Yeah? Wanna hear more?

CHRISTINE   Sure!

SCARLETT   But don't print this part in your article, right, just the crap about how noble I am copin on my own and that shit, and how good the United Church is helpin me out, all that shit right?

CHRISTINE   Scarlett, I won't print anything that you don't want me to. I despise journalists that do that kind of thing. I want you to think of me as a friend. Maybe we could even go out sometime, catch a movie, or go to dinner...

SCARLETT   Sure, if you like.

CHRISTINE   So! How did it all start with your boyfriend?

SCARLETT   It all started one night, I'd just been watching TV for sixteen hours straight, from eight in the morning, right? And that's hard on the eyes, I was bone tired. So I go to bed, I look out the window and there's no moon, right? And I lie there for hours, can't sleep, itchy, bored, just wishin I was dead, as usual, when I hear, my door open.

CHRISTINE   Were you frightened?

SCARLETT   I couldnta cared. I thought it was, you know, a guy with a knife, come to carve me up. I thought good, great, what a way to go. I laughed thinkin a Monica, she's my morning volunteer, thinkin a her comin in findin me dead – so I wait to be cut, but I don't hear nothin, nothin, I figure he's in his socks, not a sound then... he sits on the edge of my bed, and and and, and then he start... he start... he start... touchin my foot just touchin my foot so soft, and nice, and I... laugh. I laugh and laugh, and Christine, I don't think I ever laughed so long and so long in my life.

CHRISTINE   Who was it?

SCARLETT   That's the question, isn't it Chris? Who the hell is it?

CHRISTINE Did he... ever come again?

SCARLETT He come every time there isn't no moon, in like a big cat sit on the bed, and me, like a big piece of fruit,

> *Dance music starts. SCARLETT gets up.*

explodin in the heat, exploding up and out the whole night, I can MOVE when my boy comes, (*she twirls*) I am movin, I know I am, I am turnin and swishin and holdin,

> *A MAN enters. He and SCARLETT dance roman-tically around the set. He leaves her back in her chair, immobile, and exits.*

like eels, you ever seen eels? Lamprey eels, bril-liant light moving fast fast they swim from the Saint John River down to Montego Bay to spurt their young, I swim like that coloured-up, bright and fast when my boy comes, swirlin and movin in the dark no moon...

CHRISTINE Hey, is he handsome?

SCARLETT I tole you there's no moon.

CHRISTINE You mean you haven't–

SCARLETT He's my midnight man, you dick! My midnight man he is my midnight man, get it? You can't SEE night, you can't SEE when there's no moon why? Why do you think it's so big to see your boyfriend two eyes, nose, a mouth, what the diff, what the hell is the–

CHRISTINE I must go, I... have an appointment.

SCARLETT You're not gonna print that.

CHRISTINE I have a job, Scarlett, I have a child to support...

SCARLETT I'll slit your throat if ya print that.

CHRISTINE   Goodbye.

SCARLETT grabs CHRISTINE's clothing.

SCARLETT   PLEASE!! PLEASE!! Please, Christine, my old
lady and old man, they're old, my mum's had a
stroke, my dad's got MS, this'd kill em, please!!

CHRISTINE   That is not my business, Scarlett, Scarlett, let go of
me, LET GO!

SCARLETT   Reverend Pete and everybody down the church,
they'd think I was a slut, they'd send me to the
freakhouse.

They struggle.

CHRISTINE   Let me go!!

SCARLETT falls on top of CHRISTINE.

SCARLETT   You're gonna kill me, you're gonna kill me.

CHRISTINE rolls her off and onto the floor.

CHRISTINE   You are trying to obstruct the freedom of the press,
lady.

SCARLETT   You can't do this you can't do this!

CHRISTINE   (*frees herself and gets away*) I'm sorry. I'm doing it.

SCARLETT   I'll see you in hell!!

This stops CHRISTINE.

CHRISTINE   What?

SCARLETT   I said you'll go right to hell for this!!

CHRISTINE   I don't believe in hell.

SCARLETT   Joke's on you, girl, cause I'm in it, right now, live
from hell, and if you do this, you're gonna be
burning here with me, maybe not today, maybe

not tomorrow but soon, soon, you'll be whizzing down the highway with a large group of handsome friends to some ski resort or other, and your male driver will decide to pass on the right, you will turn over and over, knocking into each other's skulls breaking each other's necks like eggs in a bag, falling through windshields it's gonna rain blood and I will open my big jaws and swallow youuuu! YOU will spend the rest of eternity inside me. Inside my... body and ooooh time goes slowwwwwe...

CHRISTINE   You're crazy.

SCARLETT   I am waiting for you Chrissy, I'm waiting for you Chrissy, I am waiting for you Chrissy, I am...

CHRISTINE   STOP THAT. Stop that craziness NOW there is no such thing, there is no such thing as any of that ANY of it. You live and you die in your own body and you go up to heaven or just nowhere.

SCARLETT   Into the middle of Scarlett...

CHRISTINE   You don't know ANYTHING.

SCARLETT   Inside my big wet behind...

CHRISTINE   Stop it. Stop saying those things.

SCARLETT   In the bummy of a big dead fish...

CHRISTINE   Stop it, I said stop it now.

SCARLETT   Your left arm and your head too, Chrissy, gonna be severed you'll be all over the highway and your mean little soul will...

CHRISTINE   (*beats SCARLETT to the ground, screaming*) STOP IT! STOP IT! (*kicking her*) STOP IT! STOP IT! (*CHRISTINE collapses*)

    SCARLETT breathes with difficulty.

Oh no. Oh no. Scarlett, are you okay? You're okay. You're okay. Your mother will be by soon or a volunteer and, and I'll call, I, I, I'll call an ambulance. You shouldn't have made me do that, Scarlett. You shouldn't have made me kick you like that. The way you, you, you talked to me like that. Like, like, like you belong. In the world. As if you belong. Where did you get that feeling? I want it. I need it. (*pause, about to exit*) I need it.

SCARLETT   OOOOOOH! Come down and kiss me, put your tongue in my mouth!! Come on, NOW, RIGHT now, there's no one around, right now, on the ground, do me, kiss me, come down and kiss me, like a lion, so hot right here right now, swirl, swirl me twirl, twirl me, make me light, light exploding into... (*laughs*)

> *CHRISTINE returns, swooping down like a condor, gives SCARLETT the kiss of death. SCARLETT, thinking it is her lover, responds passionately and then, without air, dies.*

ISOBEL   (*to CHRISTINE, touching her*) SLAVE! You are a slave of the lion! You lie with him you laugh you let him bite your neck, you spread your legs. You will take me to him now.

> *Music, blackout. Lights up on CHRISTINE's office. She is moving things in an angry way.*

ISOBEL   Shhh. I wait for the lion!!

> *RODNEY, an early-middle-aged man with a stoop, CHRISTINE's research assistant, comes in and waits until she addresses him. He has an armload of papers.*

CHRISTINE   Yes, Rodney, what is it?

RODNEY   I've... uh... brought the research material you asked for.

CHRISTINE Good. Great. Thank you... how was your week-
end?

RODNEY Quiet.

CHRISTINE Rodney. Rodney – Rodney I told you I wanted
stats on CP, cerebral palsy, not just "handicapped
people." I wanted information on cerebral palsy!

RODNEY You did NOT specify cerebral palsy, Christine.

CHRISTINE Oh yes I most certainly did, I said–

RODNEY I have it on tape, Christine!

CHRISTINE Rodney! Are you or are you not a professional
researcher?

RODNEY Yes.

CHRISTINE Well then start doing professional work! NOW!
Or you are out. Is that understood? IS THAT
UNDERSTOOD?

RODNEY ...of... course...

CHRISTINE exits. RODNEY is at his desk.

You will NOT EVER SPEAK TO ME THAT WAY
AGAIN CHRISTINE YOU WILL NOT TREAT ME
AS AN OBJECT DO YOU UNDERSTAND? Is that
understood? IS THAT UNDERSTOOD??

Knock on the door.

Yes? Hello. May I help you?

MICHAEL Yes, I'm looking for a Rodney LeHavre –
I was directed to this office.

RODNEY I... am... Mr. LeHavre.

MICHAEL Rodney?

RODNEY Do I know you?

MICHAEL	Michael... Lind... from St. George's, '60 to '64. How are you? You remember me, don't you?
RODNEY	Michael... Lind? No. No, I'm afraid I don't, I'm sorry. Were you in my class?
MICHAEL	Yeah, yeah, we were good friends for a while even; don't you remember? Come on. We played chess. You were a great player. You taught me... how to play. You must remember.
RODNEY	Chess.
MICHAEL	I guess you don't remember. I'm sorry. I was sure that you'd remember. I... I... (*backing out*)
RODNEY	Would you like to come in and sit down? I can take ten minutes I think. Would you like to sit down?
MICHAEL	Oh, oh, okay, if you don't mind...
RODNEY	No. A cup of coffee... I could – get the secretary Sherry – to–
MICHAEL	(*laughs*) You've got to remember the fly collection. It was really hot. July, I think. We caught it must have been fifty house flies, and, and we stuck them with Elmer's glue, to a piece of Bristol board. To a big piece of Bristol board. And labelled them in Latin. Don't you remember? You must remember.
RODNEY	Wait a minute... wait a minute... yeah, yeah, and we even named them, didn't we? Didn't we name each one?
MICHAEL	Yeah, yeah... I'll never forget. You even named one Clarence. I thought it was brilliant.
RODNEY	Right! And yours were all names like Fred, Joe, Cindy, weren't they? Right!

MICHAEL   And yours were all royalty – Elizabeth, Margaret, Clarence. God!

RODNEY   God. A fly collection. So what did we *do* with it?

MICHAEL   I think... we had it arranged... to show someone. A colleague of my father's. Someone in insect...

RODNEY   Entomology.

MICHAEL   Yeah, that's it. And it was raining or something...

RODNEY   Pouring, yes, pouring, and all the flies–

RODNEY &
MICHAEL   –FELL OFF THE BRISTOL BOARD!

RODNEY   God. Michael Lind. Michael LIND! I'm sorry.

CHRISTINE   (*off*) Rodney I need that material as SOON as possible, please!

MICHAEL   Well I see that you have to get back to work, I'd better go... ahhh... just before I go, there's one thing. I uh... this is going to sound strange, but... I've been having... sort of... dreams... about... back then, I... have them a lot–

RODNEY   Oh?

MICHAEL   Yes, only... I always wake up at the same spot, fairly distressed, actually, and... I just... wondered... if you could... help me... remember... what actually happened. Back then... when we were... kids. Do you think you could–

RODNEY   Sure, I could try...

MICHAEL   Okay, let's start at the beginning. It was something to do with chess.

RODNEY   Chess.

MICHAEL   You loved to play chess you... brought me to your house after school, it was a Tuesday, I think, cold, we went through a short cut it said "Pedestrians Only' I thought it said "Protestants Only" and I was terrified.

RODNEY laughs.

And we went to your room, with all the paper airplanes hanging from the ceiling all over the room! And we lay on the floor. Do you remember? You remember lying on the floor? Rodney, your carpet. Your carpet was brown and orange, sort of circles or something. There was the sound of a snowblower outside. My queen. You took my queen. And then, and then, Rodney, didn't we laugh, or or or or... some touch some touch Rodney and you made a strange sound. What was that sound. Please help me! I need to go back there. I need to go back there, you see? You were the only – friend that I – we saw the world the same way. Remember? We saw the world the same way. I want to go back there. (*caresses his shoulder*) I want to go back there...

RODNEY   I want to go back there, too. I want to go back there, too.

> *MICHAEL and RODNEY embrace. RODNEY makes the sound. MICHAEL pulls him back and throws him to the ground.*

MICHAEL   QUEER!! Queer queer queer queer queer queer QUEER! FAIRY SISSY LITTLE CREEP!! DON'T YOU EVER ever remember again. YOU have WRECKED my life, your slimy memory, using me over and over and over again like an old porno magazine you will RELINQUISH that memory you will wipe it OUT, YOU understand?

RODNEY   You're crazy, you need psychiatric...

MICHAEL   You will NOT remember me again because if you do, if you do, I will feel it, oh yes, and I will come and I will kill you. I could feel you remembering, almost daily, I would be in the middle, the middle

of a crucial business meeting all the way in
Vancouver and suddenly I would feel you... holding my memory, turning it over and over, folding
it, caressing it, reliving it, SPEWING, spewing
your filth all over me. How how I always wondered how could you do it in the middle of the
day? Did you do it here, at work, at this desk is
this where you–

RODNEY   Anywhere I can, Michael. You see, my life has
been terribly disappointing.

MICHAEL   You will... free me–

RODNEY   Of course. I'll try, but memory... does seem to
have a will of its own, I can't really help what–

>   *MICHAEL hits him, they fight, rolling and punch-*
>   *ing, and end up on the floor. Very, very slowly*
>   *MICHAEL raises his head, extends his tongue,*
>   *RODNEY does the same. They come together and*
>   *their tongues touch. It is an ecstatic moment for*
>   *both of them. MICHAEL pulls out a knife, ROD-*
>   *NEY takes it from him and cuts his throat.*
>   *MICHAEL dies. Music. The actor playing*
>   *MICHAEL gets up and exits. ISOBEL goes to*
>   *RODNEY and touches him, then RODNEY gets up*
>   *and straightens himself.*

RODNEY   "Hello, welcome to St. George's. My name is
Rodney LeHavre, grade seven, and you're...?
Michael Lind! Welcome! You just came from
Vancouver? I have a cousin there! Do you play
chess?" Chess, every day... chess, Monday,
Tuesday, Wednesday, Thursday, chess, with...
Michael... at school, at my house at his house in
his room, lying on our stomachs staring at the
chess board, he sticks his tongue out at me
because he had just captured my queen and then I
stuck my tongue out back at him and he moved
forward just a bit till his tongue was touching
mine, and my whole life jumped into my tongue
we didn't move just lay there touching tongues,
"Would you boys like some tuna sandwiches?" his

mother the best mother in the world with her red
bangles and bourbon sour at six, "Okay Mrs. Lind,
thanks!" And we had a secret, an atomic secret
nobody else in the whole entire world knew that
we had touched tongues oh OH wrote his name,
MICHAEL, over and over one thousand times one
thousand times; on the fifth day, the fifth day after,
I'm at the blackboard doing math, very good at
math, superb mind for mathematics the other boys
jealous, always been jealous of my superior brain
throwing spitballs, used to that, yelling "Froggy,
froggy frog" because of my francophone name,
used to that, I turn, I catch his face white darkened
so quickly like a sky, he caught, he knew, suddenly he knew, Michael, that he had been playing
chess with the loser "FROGGY, HEY FROGGY"
they scream "HEY FROG." He stands up! They
look expectantly, is the new kid going to defend
his friend? What's he going to say, I to myself,
"Oh thank you, Michael, thank you thank you the
first to ever defend me oh what what are you
going to say to defend me?" He takes a breath,
I'm holding mine, he smiles he speaks he says: "Is
he a frog... OR A TOAD!!" They laugh and laugh
and laugh screaming their laughter slapping their
desks shaking their fists triumphing a new member of the PACK!! Is he a frog, or a toad – Am I a
frog or am I a toad?

    SHERRY enters.

SHERRY   RODDEE! RODDEEE!! Baby Bunny.

ISOBEL   She!

SHERRY   You'll never guess what I have! Milk chocolate bar
with lots of gushy cream in it. Two squares for
you, and two squares for me.

ISOBEL   She!

SHERRY	One hundred and forty calories a square who gives a shit. I heard Christine chewin ya out, what a fuckin cow.
ISOBEL	She... I see, I smell the spray, the Lion's spray...
SHERRY	(*notices that RODNEY is very upset*) What happened?

SHERRY runs from RODNEY's office back home to the apartment she shares with her boyfriend of two years, EDWARD, an out-of-work actor. When she comes in he is practising a tap routine for an audition. Newspapers are all over the floor.

SHERRY	JeSUS I'm peed off – I'm standing on the escalator, right? Goin down to the subway? My back hurts, I don't feel like takin the stairs? So I'm standin there when this woman shoves by me right into the wall and goes, "Can't *you* move? Some people are in a hurry!" And I just STAND there like a fucking WETWIPE with my mouth open FUCK if I see that bitch again–
EDWARD	That's very interesting, Sherry.
SHERRY	Whatcha workin on that dance try-out thing?
EDWARD	Uh, no. I'm fixing the faulty wiring with my feet, it's magic, Sherry, really! Right through the–
SHERRY	Ah Jeez, you're not mad at me again are ya? Whad I do now?
EDWARD	I don't know, Sherry, what did you do now?
SHERRY	I get off work at five-thirty, Ed, it's ten to six what the hell am I supposed to do? Fly home?
EDWARD	I phoned work at four o'clock, Sherry, and Arlene said that you had left for the day.
SHERRY	Oh well THAT – I was havin a coffee and a piece of cake with Rodney, he–

EDWARD   Don't lie, please.

SHERRY   I was, Eddie, ask Rodney, ask–

EDWARD   You've rehearsed them all.

SHERRY   Listen to me! Rodney had some kind of fit today,
                Christine just about called the cops he was yelling
                and screaming at nobody all afternoon – he's right
                nuts.

EDWARD   It is a skillful liar it is.

SHERRY   *Don't call me "it".*

EDWARD   I beg your pardon?

SHERRY   Have you been drinking? Or doin coke or some
                shit? You have, haven't you? You–

EDWARD   We're out of toilet paper.

SHERRY   No, there's more right under the–

EDWARD   No there's NOT!

SHERRY   Alright, I'll go and get some now–

EDWARD   YOU'LL stay right where you are, Sherry. Please.
                PLEASE I'm asking you. Don't leave me alone—
                here—I don't want to be alone.

SHERRY   Aww Eddie, you know I love you, don't you.

EDWARD   If – if you're not happy with my performance in
                bed... I wish you'd just... tell me and – and–

SHERRY   Honey, I love your performance in bed.

EDWARD   You don't really, do you?

SHERRY   Listen I was just tellin Arlene today you got the
                best hands of I bet any guy there is on the whole
                fuckin planet!

EDWARD   You were?

SHERRY   The way you touch me, Eddie, Christ, I feel like a whole bouquet, you know? A bouquet of red flowers just... poppin open, poppop pop pop pop just like on one of them nature specials. I love makin love with you, I think about it all day, half the time my pants are wet thinkin about you.

EDWARD   They're not, really?

SHERRY   They are. Feel... feel that (*puts his hand under her dress*) Oh honey I want you to make love to me. Please?

EDWARD   (*kissing her*) Oh! Oh! I've been thinking about you too, all day, every day.

SHERRY   Oh Eddie, I want you.

EDWARD   You want me...?

SHERRY   Did you not get that part in the TV series? About the runaway kid or whatever? Is that why you're – Eddie what's wrong? Did I say something wrong?

EDWARD   YOU ARE A FLAMING ASSHOLE!

SHERRY   Eddie!

EDWARD   Who are you dreaming about every night?

SHERRY   What?

EDWARD   Every night you're moaning like an animal in heat, who?

SHERRY   What?

EDWARD   Who are you dreaming about, Sherry?

SHERRY   Nobody! I'm not dreaming about – nobody.

EDWARD	WHO ARE YOU DREAMING ABOUT?
SHERRY	Just forget it, I'm going over to Arlene's, I'll see you later.
EDWARD	You tell me who you are dreaming about or I will cancel the wedding.
SHERRY	Eddie.
EDWARD	I will... TODAY, if you don't stop lying to me treating me like a fucking maggot–
SHERRY	I'm not lying to you Ed, please, just–
EDWARD	I'll cancel the wedding! I'll phone up Father Hayes and I'll cancel the whole fucking thing.
SHERRY	I paid nine hundred dollars for that dress, Eddie.
EDWARD	I don't give a flying fuck what you paid for it.
SHERRY	EDDIE my mum's got her ticket from Florida, my sisters–
EDWARD	I don't give a hot damn miss–
SHERRY	OKAY OKAY OKAY OKAY you're right, you're right. There is someone I'm dreaming about... it's... uh... it's...
EDWARD	Now we are cookin' with GAS, Sherry. This is what I always knew in my heart never DARED with all this feminist shit going down. Come on, come on tell me if I'm going to be your husband I want to know it all.
SHERRY	Tell you. Tell... you...?
EDWARD	You were walking home from the subway, yes?
SHERRY	Yes.
EDWARD	About one thirty in the morning, yes?

SHERRY	Yes. Well. I had been at my great aunts doin'–
EDWARD	I don't give a fuck where you were Sherry you were walking home, one thirty in the morning, right?
SHERRY	Right.
EDWARD	And you hear steps behind you.
SHERRY	Steps.
EDWARD	Clack clack clack like cowboy boots.
SHERRY	Clack. Clack.
EDWARD	And a voice...
SHERRY	Like a housefly.
EDWARD	A VOICE.
SHERRY	Asks me if I had been seein' that... porno show down the street.
EDWARD	And you said...
SHERRY	I didn't say, Ed, I walked faster.
EDWARD	But your heels, were so high, so provocative, that you turned on your ankle.
SHERRY	I sprained my ankle.
EDWARD	And he grabbed you.
SHERRY	By the arm!
EDWARD	He was all man.
SHERRY	Oh no! No!
EDWARD	And then what happened, Sherry? What happened then?

SHERRY   You know what happened Ed.

EDWARD   I forget, Sherry. Tell me again. Tell me again,
           come on, come ON or I... cancel...

SHERRY   You know what happened.

EDWARD   OR I CANCEL...

SHERRY   He threw me between two houses, Ed.

EDWARD   And you are breathing fast. And hot.

SHERRY   And he smashed my head against the fire wall, Ed.

EDWARD   You dream about that, don't you Sherry?

SHERRY   And he told me he was going to kill me.

EDWARD   His voice. MASTERFUL...

SHERRY   And he held my throat and he...

EDWARD   And he...

SHERRY   Please, Eddie. Please please, I am asking you... I
           can't do this again, I can not go through it for you,
           Eddie. I'm tired, I'm...

EDWARD   And? And?

SHERRY   And I fought like a cat, Ed, you know that! I
           scratched him and bit him and twisted and
           screamed but he–

EDWARD   But he...?

SHERRY   He–

EDWARD   He–

SHERRY   Eddie please...

EDWARD   Say it!!!

SHERRY   NO!

EDWARD   Say it now Sherry.

SHERRY   Eddie!

EDWARD   You *are* the snake.

SHERRY   No.

EDWARD   Because the snake tempts others to sin, uh huh? SATAN tempts others to sin. Say it Sherry. Come on, "I am the snake," come on, "I am the snake," "I am the snake" come on COME ON.

SHERRY   I... am... the snake.

EDWARD   With the diamond back, glittering.

SHERRY   Yeah. I am. The snake. With the back.

EDWARD   Oh yes!! You ARE the snake, baby, come on, "I am the snake!"

SHERRY   I am. The snake! I am the snake! I am the snake! I AM THE SNAKE I AM THE SNAKE I AM THE SNAKE I AM THE SNAAAAAAAAKE!

SHERRY breaks down in tears. She collapses on the floor. EDWARD cleans up and then sits down.

Eddie? Will you come with me tomorrow then to Ashley's to pick out a pattern? Like I've made the appointment and everything Ed, and after all, you are going to have to live with the dishes. I mean, I know guys hate goin' in there, all guys do, but everyone that gets married goes to Ashley's, everyone that gets married–

EDWARD   Alright. But nothing with flowers on it. I just want something clean, maybe – white, with a black stripe.

She thinks, changes her mind, then turns away.

> *ISOBEL enters the room, and offers her hand to SHERRY, who takes it, gratefully. Arm in arm, they walk away from SHERRY and EDWARD's apartment to a graveyard. At first ISOBEL is helping SHERRY, but by the time they reach the graveyard, it is SHERRY who helps ISOBEL find her grave, and gently lays her down, and disappears.*

NOTE: The next section has two scene options

SCENE OPTION 1:

> *In the graveyard, sitting on another tombstone, is BEN, the man who killed ISOBEL seventeen years before.*

BEN　　　　There's one thing, you know. There's one thing that I always... wanted to tell somebody and that is that... I done her a favour. I was – kindly – yeah, see, I pull her outa the car and throw her on the cement in front of the warehouse there's a streetlight and... and she says to me she says, "Please," she says, "Please no strangle, I so... scared of strangle," in this voice of breath just... purely of breath so I stopped, eh? I did. I stepped out of the twister cause that's what it's like, when you're doin something like that, you're inside a twister and to step out, is like... liftin a dishwasher, eh, but I did. So I go back of the warehouse and I picked up a brick and I hit her – cause she touched me okay? She touched me, right?

> *ISOBEL approaches with her weapon.*

SCENE OPTION 1 CONTINUES ON PAGE 73..

SCENE OPTION 2:

> *In the graveyard, a group of mourners exit, leaving BEN and his mother alone.*

JOAN   Dear, you're looking quite uncomfortable, shall we go?

BEN   Yeah, yeah, let's go. No. No. Let's stay here. Here, sit on a tombstone why dontcha? (*reading*) "Harvey J. Walker, 1920-1973." What's that make him?

JOAN   Dear, it's getting quite chilly, don't you think?

BEN   It's summer, Joanie!

JOAN   Yes dear, but there is a wind! I'm afraid my silly old hair will just–

BEN   JOAN! I wanna siddown and pay my respects. SIDDOWN! SIT DOWN!

JOAN   (*sitting down awkwardly*) All right. Somebody hasn't watered these impatiens in a very long time. Poor old Father Hayes, I will miss him.

BEN   He was an old fruit.

JOAN   Benny he was not, how can you say that about Father Hayes?

BEN   Because he talked like a fruit; he walked like one too.

JOAN   Now now, you don't mean that.

BEN   I sure as hell do.

JOAN   BEN PLEASE your language!!

BEN   So, whatdya been up to, Joan, lots a charity work, what?

JOAN   Yes, I'm still working in the shop, at the hospital.

BEN   What about bridge, you still play bridge?

JOAN	Oh yes, every week, heavens, I guess it's been every week for the last... fifteen years. Ben I wish you would call me Mum.
BEN	I can't. I told you that before.
JOAN	You are my son. We've had you since you were three weeks old for heaven's sake.
BEN	I don't give a shit. You're Joan, I like you, you're just not my mother.
JOAN	You break my heart, Christine still calls me Mum.
BEN	Christine's different.
JOAN	How? How is Christine different?
BEN	Cause... she's... like you, see; she's the same. Her mother was some kinda student or something, her father a professor or some shit, me, I wasn't from nothin, I'm different, I'm different from you, see?
JOAN	I love you Ben, I hope you...
BEN	Don't say that word.
JOAN	I'm sorry, but it's true, I love every hair on your sweet head...
BEN	Joan.
JOAN	And I will till the day I die.
BEN	DO YOU LOVE ME?
JOAN	Well yes, I just–
BEN	Do you love me?
JOAN	Terribly.
BEN	Well then gimme some money.

JOAN	I beg your pardon?
BEN	I need a loan. About sixty thousand bucks. And I need it tonight.
JOAN	Oh so that's why you agreed to come with me to Father Hayes' funeral, stupid me, I actually thought...
BEN	Shutup, I came because I knew it meant something for you, I hadn't seen you in a while–
JOAN	Eight months.
BEN	Yeah well I was busy.
JOAN	You're only seeing me because you want money.
BEN	Shutup, don't give me that shit...
JOAN	It's obviously true, Ben.
BEN	Okay, it's true. Can you get the money?
JOAN	What do you need it for?
BEN	I said can you get it?
JOAN	I don't know, Ben, I don't know until you tell me what you need it for.
BEN	Okay I'm leaving.
JOAN	Ben WAIT, WAIT. (*crying*) I'm sorry.
BEN	WELL don't cry, I hate it when an old woman cries, it's friggin gross youse are ugly enough to begin with but when you start with the water...
JOAN	Ben that's enough.
BEN	I'm just being straight, Joan, come on, the old "visage" is NOT what it used to be, HEY, you can take a little tease can't ya?

JOAN   Well I know I've aged, dear, but I didn't think–

BEN   You're old and ugly. But you're okay. Wanta
            smoke?

JOAN   No thank you Ben, you know I don't.

BEN   The cancer thing, right, right, well I don't give a
            shit myself, so I'm gonna smoke myself sick.

JOAN   Ben, why do you say you don't care?

BEN   Cause I'm a sittin duck. Unless you give me that
            cash money now, I'll be dead news anyways, so
            what do I care.

JOAN   I don't follow you, Ben.

BEN   I'm saying that there's people after me, Joanie, bad
            bad dudes, these jokers don't think nothin, nothin
            of blowin a guy's head off and stickin him in a
            trunk.

JOAN   Oh Benny how did you get involved with these...

BEN   Don't ask questions, Joanie, for crying out loud,
            I did time in a federal penitentiary, I did twenty
            years in friggin Collins Bay the place is crawlin
            with creeps they follow you out...

JOAN   Why are they... after you?

BEN   Why are they after me? Why are they after me?
            You are askin me why they are after me? Why do
            you think?

JOAN   Well goodness anybody who knows anything
            knows you did not kill that little girl, all the maga-
            zines wrote about the suppressed evidence, and
            impossibility of the time factor, everybody knows
            it was a miscarriage of justice–

BEN	I know that you know that, butcha think the turkeys know that? Hey, they just gotta feel upper than somebody, right? They're the lowest on the social ladder they gotta have somebody lower, that's me, scum of the earth.
JOAN	Oh Benny.
BEN	You never thought I done it.
JOAN	Not for a second.
BEN	May I ask why?
JOAN	Because – because – you would fall asleep only in my arms till you were six years old.
BEN	ONLY IN YOUR ARMS.
JOAN	And you brushed my hair, your favourite pastime in the world was for us to lie on the bed and you would brush and brush my hair, my hair was long then black...
BEN	I still like brushin chicks' hair.
JOAN	I always knew, I always knew it wasn't you.
BEN	I know. I know you always knew that.
JOAN	I am your mother...
BEN	NO!
JOAN	I AM.
BEN	You are not! You are... my guardian, LIKE a mother to me not my mother. My mother is probably some whore living outa Dominion bags now.
JOAN	Oh Benny.
BEN	Are you gonna give me the cash?

JOAN	Just... please, please tell me what it's for? Please darling?
BEN	Surgery. Changin my face so those jokers won't know me, then I'm gonna start in on the pasta, the milkshakes, gain fifty pounds, then dye the hair red.
JOAN	But surely that won't cost–
BEN	LET ME FINISH, Christ, did ya ever let anybody finish anything?
JOAN	I'm sorry.
BEN	You better be. Now where was I...
JOAN	About why you need so much–
BEN	Okay, after the looks change, I go into business I gotta idea for a business gonna make me a millionaire. Alls I gotta do, is have some cash up front.
JOAN	Ben, dear, I don't mean to be discouraging, but I've watched so many of these schemes of yours–
BEN	What?
JOAN	Fail!!
BEN	They didn't fail! They didn't fail they just didn't work cause of people rippin me off cause my heart was too big!! Well this time I learned my lesson I know I know to be ruthless, okay?
JOAN	Well I don't think you have to be "ruthless," I mean Walter was a brilliant business man, but he was never never–
BEN	(*spits*) HE WAS A SON OF A BITCH.
JOAN	Walter loved you, Benny.

BEN	Don't you mention that man's name the man was a pig .
JOAN	Ben you are talking about your father, my husband.
BEN	NOT MY FATHER NOT MY FATHER YOU only saw one face, Joanie one WALTER face, the other face was secret, between him and me, only I saw the...
JOAN	Oh Ben how can you–
BEN	He he he he he used to force me...
JOAN	He forced you to do what?
BEN	Well... forget it.
JOAN	Ben, please, I don't understand what you–
BEN	WHY DO YOU THINK THIS BOY IS HELL, I was hell for you from the time I was seven, killin the cats, wrecking the car, sellin your stereo WHY? Cause my mother was a fifteen-year-old kid from Gerrard and Parliament with stringy hair... who couldn't say her alphabet? You think it's that? Why do you think it is, Joanie, why do you think I am hell?
JOAN	I think that when we told you that you were adopted, you were crushed and we were never able to help you.
BEN	No. So whaddya think it is, Joan?
JOAN	...Something... Walter...?
BEN	Yeah. Yeah. Yeah...something Walter said.
JOAN	You are saying that he... did something to you – he struck you?
BEN	Joanie bein hit, I wouldn'ta minded, hell it was a relief when it was that. It's... the other...

JOAN	It's not true.
BEN	You never noticed anything, NOTHIN strange? Whyd'ja think, whyd'ja think he left the bed every night?
JOAN	To have a snack, he... always said that he had had a... snack.
BEN	(*laughs*) Yeah right.
JOAN	I'm... really in a state of shock.
BEN	Believe me, Joan.
JOAN	I thought I knew Walter so well...
BEN	Yeah.
JOAN	OH GOD. My little boy, my poor little...
BEN	Poor Joanie, no one told her. No one ever told her that 95% of the human population is maggots. You got fooled into thinkin life was nice tea parties and hot cocoa after skatin and tuckin your kids in and singing a pretty song about the fuckin moon... Member that rabbit I used to have?
JOAN	Honey.
BEN	Yeah Honey, well, Honey always made me think of you, you know, with those big wide apart eyes, believe everything thinkin everything is nice, so trusting, she was so trustin it made me mad, you know? Like why do you trust me don't you know I could pull your eyes out? You should hop away when my hands are in your cage, hop away, you stupid pest, don't just stand there. With those eyes.
JOAN	Is that why you–
BEN	I DON'T LIKE STUPIDITY.

JOAN	Oh dear.
BEN	Look, Joan, I'm short on time here, so do we have a deal?
JOAN	Sixty... thousand...?
BEN	You got it.
JOAN	Oh Ben. Oh Ben. Walter. I am shattered to know that my Walter–
BEN	Hey. Would I lie to you Joanie? Just to score some cash? Come on...
JOAN	Now I know, Ben, I know...
BEN	Whaddya know.
JOAN	Her picture, in the papers on all those posters, that picture, her eyes, she had unusually trusting, wide apart–
BEN	Back off, I'm tellin ya Joanie–
JOAN	YOU HATE TRUSTING EYES because – they reminded you of me and how... I trusted Walter, how I let it go on, how dumb I was how dumb I was, you were killing me, killing – WALTER! It's all my fault!! That little girl's death is all my fault!
BEN	There's one thing, you know. There's one thing that I always... wanted to tell somebody and that is that... I done her a favour. I was – kindly – yeah, see, I pull her outa the car and throw her on the cement in front of the warehouse there, and... I put my hands around her neck and she says to me she says "Please," she says, "please no strangle, I so... scared of strangle" in this... voice of breath just... purely of breath and I stopped, eh? I stepped out of the twister cause that's what it's like, Joanie, when you're doin somethin like that you're inside a twister and to step out, is like... liftin two hundred pounds but I did cause she touched me,

okay? She touched me right – she was me, right?
She was me, under Walter, asking him askin him
please Daddy, please, please, Daddy so I done
what I always wanted Walter to do, what I always
wished what I wished every night, I got a brick a
plain red brick, yeah, killed her with a brick,
smashed her little face in. To this day I can't watch
them Brick commercials, you know, the furniture
warehouse? No money down – turn the set right
off, right off for the night. Hey! Did I really used
to brush your hair?

> *He puts his head in her lap. She extricates herself
> and backs off in horror. ISOBEL approaches with
> her weapon.*

SCENE OPTION 1 AND SCENE OPTION 2
BOTH RESUME AT THIS POINT IN THE PLAY:

ISOBEL   BEN... ja.. men.

> *He looks.*

ISOBEL   BEN ja men BEN ja men.

BEN   Who are you?

ISOBEL   Is... o... bel.

BEN   Isobel.

ISOBEL   July. Isobel in July July the one, remember? Don't
you remember? CANADA day day for CANADA
Birthday. I selling tickets tickets on a Chrysler car,
for boys' and girls' club, one dollar fifty for a ticket. I have five tickets left. Don't you remember?
I see you in park. It is raining. In my park I ask
you "you want to buy ticket on a Chrysler car?"
You say "yes, yes, I buy all five all five tickets.
Come into my car, come into my silver car with
dark red seats, come into my car. I will give you
the money for the tickets I have the money in my
car" you said...

BEN	I'm hallucinatin.
ISOBEL	I'm Isobel.
BEN	You're a picture.
ISOBEL	I'm Isobel.
BEN	What... do you want?
ISOBEL	I have come.
BEN	What do you want?
ISOBEL	I am here.
BEN	WELL GO AWAY! You hear me? GO AWAY.
ISOBEL	(*she is about to kill him with the stick, the forces of vengeance and forgiveness warring inside her – forgiveness wins*) I love you.
BEN	NO!!
ISOBEL	*You took my last breath!*
BEN	Christ I'm sick, I'm so sick.
ISOBEL	I want back my life. Give me back my life!

> *Players enter singing a religious-sounding chorale with a sense of sadness and triumph. They place a veil on ISOBEL's head, the actor playing BEN joining them.*

ISOBEL	(*an adult now*) I want to tell you now a secret. I was dead, was killed by lion in long silver car, starving lion, maul maul maul me to dead, with killing claws over and over my little young face and chest, over my chest my blood running out he take my heart with. He take my heart with, in his pocket deep, but my heart talk. Talk and talk and never be quiet never be quiet. I came back.

I take my life. I want you all to take your life.
I want you all to have your life.

> *Players sing a second, joyful chorale, walking off.*
> *ISOBEL ascends, in her mind, into heaven. The*
> *last thing we see is her veil.*

The End

OTHER TITLES
BY
JUDITH THOMPSON

The Other Side of the Dark
Includes "The Crackwalker", "I Am Yours", "Pink",
and "Tornado" (radio).
PLCN (tpb)   0-88754-537-8 (1997) $ 18.95

Perfect Pie
PLCN (tpb)   0-88754-590-4 (2000) $ 14.95
Also in *Solo*
CHP (pb)   0-88910-449-2 (1993) $ 17.95

Sled
Nominated, Governor General's Literary Award for
Drama, 1995.
PLCN (tpb)   0-88754-517-3 (1998) $ 14.95

White Biting Dog
Winner, Governor General's Literary Award for
Drama, 1984.
PLCN (tpb)   0-88754-369-3 (1984) $ 10.95

White Sand (radio)
In *Airborne*
BLI (pb)   0-921368-22-4 (1991) $ 14.95

Available from Playwrights Union of Canada
416-703-0201   fax 703-0059
orders@puc.ca   http://www.puc.ca